Monica Ridgeway

Essential Guide to Online Learning

LAUREATE INTERNATIONAL UNIVERSITIES PUBLISHING

Published by
Laureate International Universities Publishing
7080 Samuel Morse Drive
Columbia, MD 21046
www.laureate.net

Director: Hal Pollard
Content Development Manager: Dana Battaglia
Content Acquisitions Manager: Jason Jones
Content Development Specialist: Sandra Shon
Writer: Amylia Grace
Editorial and Production Services: Hearthside Publishing Services
Cover/Interior Design: Elizabeth Gething

Printed in the United States of America

Library of Congress Control Number: 2012943920
ISBN-13: 978-0-9855867-1-3 (Paperback edition)
ISBN-13: 978-0-9855867-7-5 (VitalSource edition)
ISBN-13: 978-0-9855867-8-2 (Kindle edition)
ISBN-13: 978-0-9855867-9-9 (Nook edition)
ISBN-13: 978-1-62458-000-0 (Apple edition)
ISBN-13: 978-1-62458-001-7 (Adobe Digital edition)

First Edition (Revised)
18 17 16 15 14 / 10 9 8 7 6 5 4 3 2

Contents

About This Book

If you are holding this book, you may have already made the decision to become a student in an online academic program. You have educational goals and an online program seems to meet your needs, but you are still curious about what online learning is and what it means for you. As with every academic endeavor, getting the most out of your learning experience requires preparation, motivation, and hard work. Online learning requires all of those things and a bit more. The online learning environment encompasses new technologies and teaching tools that require different strategies for students to attain success and get the most out of their learning experience. The purpose of this guide is to help you understand this environment and apply these strategies. Think of this guide as the instruction manual for your new endeavor. It covers the basics of online education and provides practical strategies, suggestions, and tips to help you complete your program of studies and ultimately meet your education goals.

This guide is organized into an introductory chapter and four sections. **Section I: Getting Started and Tools for Success** provides a basic framework with which to approach online learning and assess the type of learner you are (learning preferences). You will be introduced to the primary learning styles and figure out concepts and suggestions to help you engage productively with your online courses. Many first-time online students initially have the misperception that online programs will be easier than on-campus programs. This is simply not true. In an online program the amount and nature of the coursework is at least comparable to that assigned in an on-campus course, if not greater. This section discusses the importance of gaining comprehension skills, getting organized, managing your time, staying motivated, and managing stress. You will discover some of the most effective online communication tools and strategies and how to create an optimal study environment for online learning. In addition, by understanding how various types of online programs work, what you will need to do to succeed, and what study habits, communication, skills, and work systems you will need to have in place, you will be in great shape to begin your course.

Section II: **Getting Familiar With Technology** will help you become familiar with technology you will likely need to use at one point or another in your online academic career. You will be introduced to the basics of connecting to and navigating the tricky waters of the Internet, the pros and cons of using different computers and web browsers as part of your online toolkit, working with hardware and software, and of protecting yourself from online threats such as viruses and pop-ups. And finally, you will learn the most common components of online courses such as Online Education Management Systems: web portals, e-mailing, online chatting and discussion boards, and gain an understanding of how to use these components to communicate effectively with instructors and classmates.

In **Section III: Completing Coursework and Following Course Requirements,** you will learn your role as an online learner and how best to work in groups. This section provides tips for how to succeed in online collaboration, group projects, and other online activities.

Section IV: Writing for the Online Environment focuses on how to help online learners enhance their writing and communication skills to ensure they are best prepared for success. It is important to remember that your writing can be even more important in online courses than in a face-to-face program since you will be required to write discussion postings, an important element of participation in online classes, rather than engaging in a verbal discussion. Since your written words speak for you, it is essential to write with clarity and purpose. In this section you will also take a look at the most commonly used citing, referencing, and formatting styles: MLA (Modern Language Association) style, APA (American Psychological Association) style, and the Chicago Manual Notes & Bibliography style (NB).

In **Section V: Finishing the Course** you will revisit all you have learned about participating in an online course and how to prepare for future courses, so you can be poised for continued success.

Remember, the key to a rewarding academic experience is in how you prepare for and participate in your courses. This guide is filled with practical tips you can implement right away to help you make the most of your learning experience. Use them as they are or adapt them to fit more closely your particular situation, needs, and academic goals.

Content Reviewers

Stacey von Berger, M.A.
Master Course Developer
Laureate Education, Inc.
Baltimore, Maryland

Benjamin Duffey, M.A.
Course Developer
Laureate Education, Inc.
Baltimore, Maryland

Jason Jones, M.A.
Content Acquisitions Manager
Laureate Education, Inc.
Baltimore, Maryland

Sheri Lundquist, M.A.
Associate Professor
University of Maryland University College—Europe
Baltimore, Maryland

Ann M. Rayner, M.S.
Director, Academic Initiatives, Institutional Quality and Integrity
Laureate Education, Inc.
Baltimore, Maryland

Introduction to Online Learning

Perhaps you use e-mail and computer spreadsheets regularly at work. Maybe you are an avid user of mobile devices. Perhaps you have only ever gone online to read the news. Whatever your experience level with computers and the online universe until now, you have chosen an academic program that is either entirely online or has an online component. That is why you have this online guide, a useful set of directions for beginning this next, important phase in your life and professional or academic career.

Congratulations for choosing to continue your education in such an innovative way. Online programs are becoming increasingly popular because of the flexibility and variety they offer. Online education makes it possible for working adults and all manner of students to work together and gain access to a quality education. While the delivery of online programs may be different from traditional on-campus programs, the amount of time and dedication it takes to be successful is the same. The reality is that it is a lot of work to be in school, especially if you have a job and/or care for others. Pursuing your education is a commitment, but well worth the effort. Your first step on the road to a successful and rewarding academic experience is to get acquainted with online learning, and understand what it means for you.

Types of Programs

Online programs are created in a variety of ways using different modalities. The three main types of online programs are synchronous, asynchronous, and hybrid programs. Understanding how each of these programs works can prepare you for how to approach your virtual classroom experience. Each type of program has pros and cons, but the important thing to remember is that there are ways to adapt to any of them.

Synchronous

Some online programs are designed to be synchronous, meaning "at the same time." In synchronous programs, the instructors and students must log into the online classroom environment at specified times and participate in the learning experience together. Instructors and students use the Internet to access an online classroom. A common online classroom experience occurs in a Learning Management System (LMS). An LMS is essentially an e-classroom that contains online tools for collaboration, such as discussion boards or chat features. It also contains tools for submitting and retrieving assignments, and for recording grades. Blackboard Inc. is a common LMS that can be used in a synchronous class. Other virtual classroom technologies include chatrooms, webcasting, instant messaging, and telecasts or teleseminars.

Although still a "virtual" classroom experience, synchronous programs more closely mimic a traditional face-to-face classroom experience because all program participants are expected to meet online at the same time using the same technology. Synchronous programs take place in real time and allow instructors to offer "live" lectures and discussions. Students can participate in real time question and answer (Q&A) sessions, lively class discussions and debates, and group projects. They are able to receive an immediate response to their questions and concerns.

Asynchronous

If you have ever followed a neighborhood e-mail list or discussion thread, you have seen how a conversation that is not in "real time" can evolve. This is one example of an asynchronous exchange. An asynchronous class means students are not required to log into the class together at the same time. Many online courses are asynchronous. A distance learning or correspondence course is another type of asynchronous course because assignments are mailed to the instructor, assessed, and then returned to the student via postal mail.

While due dates are firm in an asynchronous course, students are free to work through weekly course material at times that work best for them. Assignments and activities are usually due by set days, by week, or within a specified period within the term. Students are free to log into the classroom according to their schedule, provided they understand the deadlines and submit work in time to meet all the requirements of the course. Some students might log in first thing in the morning, while others use their lunchtime and evening hours to access course materials online. The choice is the students'.

With the increased demand of modern lifestyles, it is easy to see why such programs are proliferating in the world of online education. However, what this means is that you need to know how to organize your time for schoolwork effectively in order to succeed.

Hybrid

Hybrid programs with a combination of delivery and participation modalities are becoming increasingly common. A hybrid is simply the combination of two or more things. In this case, hybrid programs use a combination of technologies and delivery methods to provide students with optimal learning opportunities. Many hybrid programs consist of some face-to-face instruction combined with online components such as e-classrooms, telecourses, virtual chatrooms, and other e-tools. Hybrid programs appeal to students because such programs aim to strike a balance between reaching the desired program goals, giving students the freedom and flexibility their busy lives demand, and setting students up for success.

TABLE 1. ONLINE PROGRAMS: PROS AND CONS

	PROS	CONS
Asynchronous	Can "attend" class at optimal times	Limited "live" interactions
Hybrid	May provide a variety of experiences to meet program requirements	Requires greater flexibility to manage both face-to-face and asynchronous instruction
Synchronous	Mimics bricks and mortar classes with "live time" interactions	Must "attend" class at set times without flexibility

Technology Tips

As an online student, your computer is essentially your classroom. Technology, from computer hardware to software, is necessary to complete your coursework and to participate in your class no matter the school or program. Institutions can use different LMSs to deliver courses, such as Blackboard Inc. or Moodle™. You do not need to be a computer genius to take an online course. Learn about the basic technology requirements of your institution and program as your first step. Your institution will have technology support services to help you get up and running and to navigate your virtual classroom. (See Section II for more information on technology needs.)

Do not be afraid to ask for help. Time wasted sorting out technical issues can be your enemy in an online program.

Online Communication: Reading, Writing, and Responding

A basic fact of online learning is that it requires more reading and writing than brick-and-mortar programs. As the student, you are frequently reading other students' comments, writing answers to discussion questions, and completing other written assignments.

Consider the ways in which you communicate in an online environment compared to a face-to-face class. In the latter, you may have in-class discussions or simply pose a question to your instructor that is addressed during a lecture period. In online classrooms, students and instructors communicate using chatrooms, e-mail, instant messaging (IM), and discussion boards. Likewise, many assignments are completed using these methods. In particular, discussion threads and boards are used extensively in many online programs. (See Section III for more about discussion threads and boards). You may wonder if the same type of video conferencing you use with family or at your place of employment is available in an online class. That technology may be a part of your program, but the majority of your communications, including the asking of questions, the discussions, or the delivery of assignments, will require writing.

Communicating online can be tricky. You have to choose your words carefully or your message could be misinterpreted. Note that all of your writing is being read and assessed by your instructor and fellow classmates, not just your research papers or written assignments. While you may not have to adhere to a style guide such as American Psychological Association (APA) to answer a discussion question as you would for a scholarly paper, you should remain professional and use proper grammar and punctuation in all of your written communications. (See Section IV for more information on style guides and writing scholarly papers.)

In addition to completing the course requirements, interacting with your fellow students via chat, e-mail, or IM can help you make the most of your student experience. You do not need to feel isolated simply because you are operating in a virtual environment. Remember, you are still part of a learning community, and you may make lifelong connections. Stay in touch with your classmates.

Being a student takes commitment and hard work whether you choose a face-to-face, synchronous, asynchronous, or hybrid program. But the online environment in particular provides many challenges that may be new to you. These challenges are balanced to a great extent by the flexibility online learning offers.

Remember that the quality of your education depends a great deal on how you prepare for and participate in your courses. In the new, exciting world of online education, what that means may not be apparent to you or your classmates. You will likely find that some strategies from the "old days" still apply. But new technologies, tools, and ways of approaching your education require new or adapted strategies for success. The purpose of this guide is to help you identify and apply those strategies. Think of this guide as the instruction manual for this new endeavor in your life. It covers the basics of online education and also contains practical strategies, suggestions, and tips to help your start feel a little smoother. The next step begins with you.

Section I: Getting Started and Tools for Success

Getting started in your online program takes preparation and a little research. Understanding who you are as a student and how to interact in an online program are critical steps in your preparation. Likewise, taking the time to create a study environment that will give you the space you need to work without distractions and allow you to focus on your studies will help you in the first course and throughout the program. A little preparation can take you a long way toward success.

Learning Styles

Remember part of your job as a student is to learn to adapt to your learning environment. Just as you had to adjust to different teachers and teaching styles throughout school, you will have to adjust to the type of online program in which you are enrolled. Understanding your learning style can make the adjustment easier. Your learning style is the way you prefer to learn. It does not have anything to do with how intelligent you are or what skills you have learned; learning styles refer to how your brain works most efficiently to learn new information. Many of us have more than one preferred learning style and embrace a more hybrid approach to learning. Odds are that your preferred learning styles have been with you since you were born. You can find ways to apply your learning style to each situation.

Learning styles are most often broken down into five categories. The acronym VARK, coined by Fleming and Mills (1992), can help you remember them. VARK stands for Visual, Aural/Auditory, Read/Write, and Kinesthetic sensory learning styles. Multimodal is considered a fifth learning preference, which is some combination of the four VARK styles.

Visual (V)

A Visual (V) learner comprehends best when able to see graphic representations in lieu of written or spoken words. These learners prefer information to be broken down into various types of diagrams, graphs, and flow charts. Another word to label a preference for visual learning could be Graphic (G) learning, since graphic representations of concepts are at the core of this style and this describes the method of delivery. In the online learning environment, the instructor will use graphic presentations such as PowerPoint® and video clips as teaching tools, but it is the students' obligation to use their learning style to absorb the information.

If you are a visual learner, consider creating visual explanations or graphics on your own to help you understand the course materials. You do not have to be an artist. If you are reading an article for your online course, you may want to create a simple graph, schematic, or table to highlight the key points. Or, you can print out course materials and highlight them to create a visual map of the key points.

Aural/Auditory (A)

Think of Auditory (A) learners as responding best to information that is "heard or spoken." An A learning style includes a preference for absorbing information via lectures, discussions, and audio recordings. Auditory learners sometimes read or paraphrase information out loud so they can hear themselves say it. It may appear that this learning style does not work as well in the online environment because most of the course materials are written or graphic in nature. Consider, however, that talking to your classmates in your online community can be a productive way to process the material.

Read/Write (R)

Think words, words, words. A Read/Write (R) learning style favors writing (and reading) essays, reports, written assignments, and note taking. This learning style works well in both the physical and online classroom. Participation in any educational program requires a lot of reading and writing. Well-worn tools in an R learner's toolbox include journals and notes, PowerPoint slides, lists, diaries, dictionaries, thesauri, quotations, and writing as a way to process information. It is important to note that while our online experience is rapidly changing the way we access information with the advent of Twitter®, podcasts, v-logs (video blogs) and more, the Internet relies heavily on text. Think read, read, read.

Kinesthetic (K)

Kinesthetic (K) learners learn by doing and benefit from examples that are based in reality (Fleming & Mills, 1992). Popular tools in a K learner's toolbox include demonstrations, simulations, and practical applications. The key is the practical application and personal (sometimes physical) involvement. If it can be touched, tasted, or felt, it likely appeals to K learners. In many online programs, practicums or supervised real-world applications are part of the educational experience. This is where a K learner will thrive.

Multimodal (MM)

Multimodal (MM) learners prefer to use a combination of learning styles. Realistically, there are few instances where only one learning style can be used to absorb all of the required information. Actually many of us respond well to MM learning experiences. You can choose a single mode to suit the occasion or situation, and use multiple modes to comprehend a concept more completely.

The important thing to remember about learning styles is that they provide a framework to help you understand why you might succeed in one type of course versus another. Knowing how you learn best can help you structure your study time, approach your assignments more efficiently, and produce positive results.

TABLE 2. TYPES OF LEARNING STYLES

LEARNING STYLE	MEANING
V – Visual	Prefers graphic representation of information such as graphs, illustrations, schematics.
A - Aural/Auditory	Prefers to listen and discuss. Learns from oral communications such as lectures, discussions, and recorded content.
R – Read/Write	Prefers textual information. Learns by reading, taking notes, creating lists, and referring to written resources.
K - Kinesthetic	Prefers hands-on involvement and practical applications.
MM- Multimodal	Prefers a combination of learning styles.

The decision to enroll in any educational program is a serious one. Therefore, it is normal to approach the world of online learning with some degree of trepidation. You may wonder if you will really like your online program and question whether you truly have what it takes to succeed online. While certain skills and a degree of comfort with technology are important, your skill set is only part of the equation. Your mindset is of equal importance. This includes motivation, environmental influences, and habits. There are online readiness surveys to help you assess your readiness level. Check your school's web page. These surveys will help you to asses where you are now and where you need to be to do well in most online programs.

Acquiring Necessary Skills

Students initially have the misperception that online programs will be easier than on-campus programs. This is simply not true. In an online program the amount and nature of the coursework is comparable to that assigned in an on-campus course.

The amount of reading and writing online students are required to do is quite extensive. You will write more than you would in a traditional brick-and-mortar style classroom program. This is because you have to write out all of your responses and thoughts instead of engaging in a typical verbal discussion of topics and points covered throughout your program. Necessary skills you will need are active listening and reading, pre-reading strategies, communication, and comprehension skills.

Comprehension requires you not only to understand words or concepts, but also to make connections between ideas and prior knowledge, and connect a text or situation to your life experiences. Comprehension requires you to construct meanings and negotiate those meanings in dialogue and discussion with others. In this context comprehension can be tough to define because it involves a variety of aspects of thinking and metacognition.

Comprehension Skills

While reading comprehension is important, comprehension skills encompass more than reading something and understanding it. It also involves metacognition, or thinking about your thinking. The main purpose of comprehension skills and strategies is ensuring students make sense of whatever it is they are learning, reading, or doing. Many comprehension methods are used in an interrelated manner, and although distinctions are sometimes made between strategies and skills, both terms are commonly used interchangeably. Examples of comprehension skills are understanding and analyzing the point of view of an author or person, comparing and contrasting, being able to put events in proper sequence, understanding cause and effect, and being able to classify and categorize things, events, or scenarios. These skills are often developed and strengthened through the asking of well-thought-out questions, drawing inferences from readings and surroundings (context clues), thinking ahead and predicting what may come next, and skimming for content and summarizing material.

The importance of proficiency in comprehension skills cannot be overstated. In fact, research has shown that students who take the time to build a strong foundation in comprehension by focusing on listening, reading, and communication skills (dialoging and offering/receiving feedback) are more likely to experience greater academic success than those who do not build up their comprehension muscles (Carnevale, 2002).

Active Listening

When we communicate with others face-to-face, we can gain insight into the conversation by watching others' body language and facial expressions. In an online environment you will not have that advantage, so it will be up to you to hone your active listening skills. Whether partaking in an online discussion, webcast, "live" chat, or phone call, being an active listener is essential. Being an active listener means that you are mindful and give your full attention to the present moment and what the person is saying. Good active listeners prepare for the discussion or exchange in advance. If you approach the discussion, lecture, or dialogue with a positive attitude that shows you are ready to truly engage with the material and speaker, you are more than halfway there.

The following tips will help you hone your active listening skills and enhance your comprehension:

- Quit all activities unrelated to the topic or discussion beforehand.
- Clear your mind of clutter. Listening takes place in the mind, not just the ears. Be sure you are not distracted with a bunch of "to-dos" or worries while you are trying to actively listen to the speaker or partake in the discussion, whether verbal or written.
- Review mentally what you already know about the subject and what you hope to know by the end of the exchange.

- Organize previous discussions, lectures, readings, web sites, and relevant experience beforehand so you can access all you already know while you are listening to new material.
- Avoid distractions (turn off the TV and radio, close the blinds if needed) and sit down.
- Let the discussion, argument, or presentation finish organically. Wait to form an opinion.
- Shy away from agreeing or disagreeing right away. Analyze or dissect the thought process behind what is being said instead of taking sides.
- Remember that, for the moment, you are present to listen to what the instructor, guest speaker, or classmates have to say, not the other way around.

Active Reading

In order to improve your reading comprehension skills, you need to read with intent. The intent is the purpose and framework for the reading. Do not just dive in and start reading mindlessly. Instead, practice focusing on the larger purpose and intent. In other words, figure out the why and what of what you are reading before you begin.

By being concise and setting a clear intent for why you are reading, you will be in a much better position to extract the information you need from the passage, article, or book. You will also retain the important information without much effort. Thinking about what you are reading and why helps you become an active reader. This is the polar opposite of haphazardly grabbing a book, flipping it open to the first page, and mindlessly reading. You are seeing the words on the pages, but you are not really paying attention to them.

You will be amazed at the difference a minute can make. Taking even 60 seconds to prepare yourself for the reading will make a huge difference if you are used to just diving in without thinking about what you are doing (or why). Think about what the assignment is and why your instructor assigned this particular reading. Take a minute or two and reason it out. Use this time to skim the selection and discussion questions, and glean information from the title, authors, preface, table of contents, or even the footnotes at the end. Frame your mindset and prime your brain to better comprehend the information it is about to delve into.

Knowing your learning style really helps you to understand and assimilate readings and information. If you are a visual (charts and graphs) learner, consider making charts to see the information more clearly. If you are auditory dominant, try reading aloud to yourself so you can hear as well as see what you are reading.

Pre-reading Strategies

The following tried and true pre-reading strategies are simple, yet effective. Engaging in these activities before you read should vastly improve your reading comprehension if you are not used to doing them beforehand. Here are but a few of the many strategies that can aid in reading comprehension. Go ahead and try the strategies in the list below and see if you cannot find one that works best for you.

- **Look around.** A text extends beyond the words on a page. Silly as it sounds, do take the time to notice the title. If there is a cover, take a look at it. Check out who authored the book, text, or article. Notice what year it was published. All these little details help you to know what to expect. It is like a puzzle. You are piecing together the outer frame first. You will piece together the whole picture later.
- **Peek inside.** Do not feel like it is "cheating" to dig into the text or story a bit and see what you can find. What can you learn by first flipping quickly through the pages and glancing at the table of contents? If it is a textbook, the table of contents can be invaluable. Right from the beginning readers are presented with a ton of information that will help frame your reading and get some sense of what is to come. The table of contents also places a singular article or chapter into a larger context.
- **Make it relevant to you.** Let us face it: Our brains are much more likely to take in and remember information if it relates to us somehow. If you can apply what you are reading to your life or interests, you will remember it a lot more easily. If you can find even one aspect of a book or reading that interests you personally or that you can relate to in some way, you are going to have a better experience with the reading, your comprehension will improve, and you will remember it a lot longer.
- **Write it down.** Now that you have a framework of expectations around what you are about to read, note passages that resonate. Jot down questions you have and observations you make that might help you

figure out the broader context or predict what is to come later on. The physical act of writing down what you are thinking or what you notice is much more powerful an act than simply thinking the thoughts in your mind and telling yourself you will remember them. Odds are you will not. Write in the margins or in a notebook and really engage with the text. True engagement starts with pre-reading. You begin to set the framework and become an active reader even before you read that first sentence.

Strong communication and comprehension skills along with your reading, writing, listening skills are the pillars to your academic success in your online learning program.

Communication

Being a good communicator is so important. In many ways, becoming a consistent and skilled communicator will be the key to your success. You, your instructor, and colleagues may not have the luxury of face-to-face communication, and all the nuance and body language cues that go along with it. You should be sure to take some time to proofread what you have written before sending e-mails or posting comments and assignments. Make it a priority to stay in regular contact with your instructor during the term. Feedback is an important aspect of online communication.

An online class is the perfect venue for you to start getting into good habits like these.

Giving and receiving constructive, prompt, and specific feedback is absolutely essential to student progress in online programs. This includes instructor feedback as well as peer feedback. Without the face-to-face components, the only real connection you have to your peers and your instructor is through consistent, written communication and regular, substantive feedback. According to studies, receiving feedback tends to be even more important in online environments than it is in traditional face-to-face programs (McVay Lynch, 2002; Palloff & Pratt, 2001). Without ample feedback, students in online programs are more likely to disconnect from the material (some even quit the program) than students attending traditional face-to-face courses (Ko & Rossen, 2001).

Know Your Role

Once you enroll in an online program, you have become a cyber-citizen of an online community. As a member of this community, you must follow an informal set of guidelines for online behavior called Netiquette. Netiquette can be summarized by three simple precepts: remember there is a human being on the other end of your communication, treat that human being with respect, and do not transmit any message that you would not be willing to communicate face-to-face. The following communication do's and don'ts should be followed in any online program, and will help you make a good impression on your instructor and your class:

1. **No Flaming**

   Flaming is the practice of insulting, not respecting, or attacking another person. Expressions of hostility are different than disagreeing with what someone says. It is okay to disagree, but it is important to do it politely. Here is an example elucidating the difference: Flaming: "Your idea is so stupid that it makes me sick. However, I'm not surprised. You seemed like an idiot on the first day of class, and I guess first impressions don't lie." Polite disagreement: "I disagree with what you have said. My experience has been different. Here's my point of view. What do you think?" Which one would you prefer?
2. **No Inappropriate Language**

   No swearing. No offensive language. No racist or sexist comments or jokes, veiled or otherwise. No general statements about gender, sexual orientation, personal beliefs, and so on. Keep it clean.
3. **No Harassment**

   Remember that the law still applies in cyberspace. Do not commit illegal acts online, such as libeling or slandering others; and do not joke about committing illegal acts. Do not misuse personal information of classmates such as e-mail addresses, etc. Respect appropriate boundaries put forth by the instructor and others.

4. **No Misuse of Class Communications**

   Do not post irrelevant messages, referred to in hacker's jargon as spam. Postings you make should only be on the topic being addressed. Do not include personal information or things shared by others in confidence unless you have asked permission to do so. Be sure your posts contribute to the discussion and offer something of value related to the topic(s) at hand. Only include relevant information, and always read all existing postings carefully before responding so you do not repeat what has already been said.

5. **No Shouting**

   Avoid putting words in all capitals. Online, all-caps is considered SHOUTING. Do not do it.

6. **Show Respect**

   Understand the importance of the concept of intellectual property. Intellectual property rights are a serious matter and it starts with being respectful of other people. Do not post, display or otherwise provide access to materials belonging to others. No using another's password; no trespassing in another's folders, work, or files. Be sure not to take someone else's ideas or thoughts and post them as your own. Be aware that to post or state something without giving credit to the person or people who came up with the idea, whether copyrighted, published, or not may not be acceptable. Even information you "borrow" from a casual conversation with others should be attributed to the proper source to avoid violating another person's sense of intellectual property rights. Be safe, not sorry. Check with your instructor or your institution about the policy.

Incorporating these guidelines into your everyday interactions with your instructor and class will help establish you as a respectful and important part of cyberspace and the online community in your program.

For more detailed information on intellectual property rights and rules, visit the website http://www.wipo.int/about-ip/en/iprm/ to download and read *The Intellectual Property Handbook: Policy, Law, and Use.*

Online instructors are trained in the art and skill of providing feedback to students. Examples of expected feedback include comments and responses to message board posts; responses to posted assignments by peers; reflection and posted responses to public instructor feedback and questions; feedback on peer reading responses; posted peer papers; and thoughts, reflections, and feedback on discussion questions and peer responses to those discussion questions.

Ideally online instructors respond promptly and provide feedback to all students quickly and mindfully. As you may already know, being able to receive useful instructor and even peer feedback is essential to continued academic progress and deep engagement with the program. Not surprisingly then, instructor feedback is frequently cited as the main catalyst for student learning in online programs. But feedback goes both ways. If you are not getting enough feedback from your instructor, it is your responsibility to let the instructor know.

The foundation to feedback in an online environment is made up of five main components:

1. Feedback should be prompt, timely, and thorough.
2. Feedback should be ongoing, formative (about online discussions and threads), and summative (about grades and assessment).
3. Feedback should be constructive, supportive, and substantive.
4. Feedback should be specific, objective, and individual.
5. Feedback should be consistent.

This may sound overwhelming, but you and your instructors and peers cannot be expected to be online around the clock. Just remember in order to achieve and maintain this high-level quality feedback (from both instructors and peers) in online programs, participants need to commit to investing a significant amount of time and effort on the endeavor.

Your written responses are the primary means of assessing your participation in the program. While it is not necessary to be a fast typist, if you are a "hunt and peck" typist or simply slower when you type, you will need to schedule extra time for completing written assignments and responding to messages and posts. Do not worry, you will get better and faster the more you do it.

Creating a Study Environment

With online programs, you take part in the class from the comfort of your own home (or office, or café). And while most students love the freedom this provides, you may go crazy trying to study and work from home. You may sit at the computer with only the best intentions to pay attention and be productive. Suddenly you begin to see *all* the things around the house that also need to be done, for example, the laundry. You may think you can do the laundry and your class work.

I'll spend an hour on this reading before posting my assignment (it's not due until midnight anyway). Then, I'll go throw some laundry in. Then, well . . . maybe I'll throw a load in now so the washer is running while I'm reading and I don't have to trek downstairs in the middle of it and be interrupted. Then, I can read and will probably need a break in a bit so I can throw the load in the dryer so it can dry while I'm working on my assignment.

. . . but multitasking is not a good practice when working on your class readings or assignments.

And even though you do your best to set aside all those distractions while you are working on school work, they nag at you from the corners of your mind. All these "to-do's" make you lose your concentration and gnaw away at you. It is a pervasive pattern that does not exactly lend itself to focused attention and high productivity. So what is the solution?

Being able to "attend" your online program from anywhere is a double-edged sword. In an online program, you do not have a specific physical classroom to go to that clearly sends a message to you and all around to you that you are in school mode. Because of this, you will have to be adamant about carving out not only sacred study times, but also your own effective study environment. It is a good idea to create a space, whether tiny or grandiose, to indicate to others that this is your study space—and time. Such boundaries are important when you are serious about getting work done and making progress in your online program.

The makeup of your study environment will depend on your own habits and preferences, as well as your lifestyle and learning style. For example, working from home can be tough if you have a family or undone chores tugging at you. In this case, you might prefer studying at a café, bookstore, or library with Wi-Fi. Perhaps the change of pace and steady stream of people energizes you. Perhaps being away from the chores with only your laptop and program materials keeps you on track. Maybe the extra shots of espresso help with focus. For others, a public environment like a café or bookstore can be an unwelcomed distraction, making it hard to concentrate and get "in the zone" for learning. Only you can know what works best for you.

One thing is certain: creating an effective study environment is not a luxury. Take this task seriously because it truly is a necessity for online students. Make sure your study space works well for you and is clean, organized, and well lit. You do not want to be distracted by clutter and disorganization. Not only does it help you take your studies seriously, increase focus, and maintain boundaries, it is also a helpful time management tool.

Ideally you would have a room or office space that is all yours. This is not always possible with family and roommates so you might consider claiming an underutilized part of your home. Some students work from the basement, attic, or even a big closet. Once you create an organized and effective study space free of distractions, you will find it is much easier to get "in the zone" more easily. You will not waste your time trying to find books and materials, or tending to the requests of others. This will create a ripple effect in your life and support you in efficiently completing your assignments and online obligations more quickly. It should also help you to absorb them on a deeper, more lasting level.

Try designating primary and secondary study spaces. Whether working from home, the office, or a public space, decide which will be the main place to complete your work for your online course, and which is an alternate. You may decide that one place is better for when you need to log in to your online course and complete online tasks. Another may be more suited to sitting and reading materials and completing offline tasks. The study space you prefer is likely one that helps you by eliminating distractions and making you feel good while you work.

To help you reduce or eliminate interruptions or distractions while you study, consider incorporating the following tips into your routine:

- Do not answer e-mail until your study time is finished.
- Allow any phone calls to go to voicemail, or turn off your cell phone. Same with text messages.
- If you use an instant messaging system, set your availability to Busy or Study Time.
- Hang a "Do Not Disturb" sign on your door or desk.
- If you use a shared electronic calendar system, such as Outlook®, set blocks of study time on your calendar so people know not to schedule meetings during that time. If you are working at home, make sure your household members know when you begin your study time.
- Consider having a calendar the household can see in which you write your study time on it, like an appointment. That way they know not to disturb you during that time.
- Establish a study ritual. For example, many students find it useful to have a little ritual they perform at the beginning of their study sessions that helps signal to them and to those around them—that it is time to study. This may include ringing a bell, brewing a fresh cup of tea or coffee, or simply arranging your "tools" on your desk, and taking out the books or materials needed for the class (Walden Student Readiness Orientation, 2012).

Getting Organized

One of the biggest challenges faced by online students is organizing and managing their time. The importance of being organized in your studies (and your life) cannot be overstated. Organizing your day in such a way that allows you to address the most important tasks that require your attention is essential. This kind of organization requires daily planning.

As an online learner, your day-to-day schedule for your program is going to be arranged differently than a traditional student's. If you were attending a traditional university with a physical campus, chances are that, in addition to your study time at home, you would spend time driving to campus, parking, walking to class, sitting in class for hours, walking back to the car, and finally driving home and unpacking your stuff. The hours add up quickly.

Although you skip much of the headache of commuting, there are things you will need to do to prepare yourself for an online program. Before you begin your program, it is important you install all hardware and software needed for your program as well as any additional tools needed for specific courses (listed in course syllabi). By installing the programs and software you will need on your computer well in advance of the start date of the program you assure yourself peace of mind. This is especially important if you are not exactly tech-savvy. Before beginning your program, you will want to check for bugs and ensure the programs are running properly. This will also give you time to familiarize yourself with the software. (See Section II for more detailed information on technology.)

You may have chosen online learning because it appears to offer the convenience and flexibility of schedule you could not get at a traditional university. And, because there is no traveling to and from campus or sitting in class, you might associate online learning with saving time.

What you need to remember is that, as an online student, the time you save by not attending a traditional university is time you spend on other tasks online. For example, the hour you save by not driving is an hour you spend reading Discussion postings in the online classroom. The 30 minutes you save by not walking between the parking lot and the classroom is 30 minutes you spend reading the weekly introduction, weekly learning objectives, and the list of weekly resources. Overall, the total hours per week for traditional learning and online learning may be similar.

Organizing Your Days

There are five keys to getting (and staying) organized in order to achieve top quality work in a highly efficient manner. You might be surprised to find that honing your organizational and time management skills has very little to do with "adding" things to your repertoire (people, skills, systems, routines, etc.). The secret to your success is actually the complete opposite of what most students think. Instead of adding more to your life, your focus will be on eliminating things.

Try the following steps for improving focus, organization, and time management skills:

1. Curb Attention Thieves. Focus on the task at hand and avoid distractions.
2. Identify time and energy wasters and eliminate them. These things suck your energy and time because they are left undone or not yet begun.
3. Create and maintain an updated to-do list. Keep track of must-do's and time for completion. Check them off as you complete them. Review your list often.
4. Finish top priority items first. Which things must be done this week? Which part needs to be completed before beginning the others?

It sounds simple enough, right? Most of us have learned that simple is not necessarily synonymous with easy. This seems especially true when we are talking about cultivating new habits or tweaking old ones. The key here is guarding your time and energy, and then using them well.

This is not an overnight process. As you progress, see how it feels to be free of many of the things that previously commanded your time and attention. The foundation here is in cutting back or eliminating all the things that divert your focus, interfere with your ability to work, and ultimately get in the way of your success.

Managing Your Time

Successful online learners need to be self-driven and motivated to complete coursework without the physical presence of an instructor and their peers. Time management and organization are essential to learning online. Despite modern time-saving conventions, our time seems increasingly limited. However, it is still possible to carve out time for the things you need to do to succeed in your online program. Try to create a realistic schedule and honor it. It is important to understand that a substantial time commitment is required every week during your course to engage in online discussions, view lectures, read course materials, post discussions, and complete assignments.

See if you can picture the following scenario: you are home all day and there is nothing in the pantry or refrigerator. You open the door. Poke around. Hum a little tune and look again. You sigh. Grab a handful of peanuts. You go back to your desk. Forty five minutes later, you are hungry, so you go back to kitchen and double-check the pantry, the cupboards, and the fridge. Nothing new has appeared.

You grab a couple handfuls of grapes, put them in a bowl, and go back to your desk. You think to yourself, "I should really go out and get something for lunch." But you do not. Some part of you knows a solution will appear. Maybe a chef will arrive at your door, armed with goodies. Or a neighbor will bring over noodle casserole. Amazingly, this does not happen.

Soon enough you are back in the pantry. You gaze at the shelves. Then, you stalk out, head to the freezer, and pull out some ice cream and sneak a spoonful. It is enough. For now. But what is really going on here?

You can see that what keeps happening in this arrangement is that you snack all day, but never feel satisfied. By 4 p.m. you are out of sorts and restless. You cannot focus and wonder why.

Here is the point: You ate. But you never actually fed yourself. Many of us do this all the time. And the very same thing happens to your attention. You have a vague notion of what you want. You roam around and surf the Internet, clicking from one thing to the next. You sit at work and putter. Return some e-mails. You get the picture.

Many people are dabblers. Dabblers do a little bit of this and a little bit of that. If you are a dabbler, you work on random things, often going for what is right in front of you instead of making a plan of action and sticking to it. You are busy, but do not commit to any one thing. This common modern affliction can be called *"Attention Thievery."* It is when you mindlessly and half-heartedly allow yourself to be distracted by nonproductive activities. You are busy and feel overwhelmed. This may be true, but not always for the reasons you think.

Curbing Attention Thieves

When Attention Thievery strikes, we let ourselves be pulled in many different directions. We are busy, but not productive. We have not chosen which things are most important to us and then made those things a priority. We are easily distracted. We answer e-mails all day long. We pick up our phones whenever they ring. It feels like we cannot stop it. But we can choose to create something different instead. Create a schedule and stick to it. Honor your priorities. Lack of focus and attention is the result of our distractions, not the cause.

Often, we start going a million miles a minute without taking time for us. When we do not consciously think about what we are doing beforehand, we get caught up in non-activities and other people's "stuff" instead of tending to our own. But our days do not have to stay that way. Though

Attention Thievery may be the norm these days, it is a curable affliction. The good news is that no matter how busy we become, we can find ways to channel our focus and energy. We just need to know how. Start with First AID: Awareness, Intention, and Dedication. Having the awareness to know when you are losing focus and getting distracted is the first step. Notice it and then set the intention to do something else.

If you are not vigilant about carving out time for the things that matter most in your day, these Attention Thieves will continue to lead you astray. Especially if you are trying to read an assignment and cook dinner while the kids are tugging at you to play or help with homework, or you have just gotten home from a long day at work and cannot escape the buzz of your cell phone and the tug of daily chores to be completed before you can feel at ease.

If focusing on one thing at a time seems impossible and counterproductive in today's multitasking world, ask yourself how many things or people you can honestly give your full attention to at a time? (Hint: It is one.) You might simply remind yourself that sometimes it is okay to take a little time for yourself. It can be healthy to take an evening off from tending to others, or your cell phone and e-mail. It can help to take time away from the computer for a day or two because all that instant communication also equals instant distractions.

Remember that your attention ultimately nourishes you. It feeds your mind and your soul, which is why it is so important to notice what you are giving your attention to. This is also why those Attention Thieves leave you and those around you unfulfilled. You nibble on this and that. You are there, but you are not. You eat, but you never actually nourish yourself. If you believe that you (and the people and goals you are committed to) deserve better, this next section will help you get there. In school, as in all areas of life, if you want to succeed it is important to learn and then use necessary skills, habits, and systems to help you reach—or even surpass—your goals.

Staying Motivated

Temptation, Distraction, and Other Pitfalls

Wanting to be motivated and making a commitment in your mind to succeed is not enough. Studies show that even when we have great intentions, even when we really do want to change, we still fail to stay motivated enough to make lasting progress about 50-80% of the time (Babauta, 2009).

There are many reasons for this. Temptation and a waning willpower are two major culprits.

Temptation is all around us. It is tempting to watch TV with our family rather than sit down in front of the computer and log on to class. It is easier to tackle mindless chores than it is to write an academic response paper.

We often think of temptations as guilty pleasures. In reality, anything desirable that conflicts or comes between you and your goal (here: succeeding in your online program) is a temptation. You can identify temptations by two main attributes:

1. Temptations are easier or more automatic than your goal.
2. Temptations are more immediately gratifying than your goal.

Long-term goals, such as succeeding in and completing your online program, can be really gratifying. However, the temptation that pulls at us is easy and gratifying right now. That is where willpower comes in. We use our willpower to battle temptation.

Willpower is the ability to put off what you want to do in this exact moment. It is the exertion of control over you, by yourself. We need willpower any time we want to change the way we would otherwise think, feel, or behave. We need willpower to follow rules and delay gratification. Willpower and self-control are the capacity to control yourself regardless of what you would rather being doing right this moment. And we use a bunch of it day in and day out.

What follows are some tried and true strategies for compensating when your willpower is low:

1. Use incentives/rewards to stay on track. Treat yourself to that movie you have been wanting to see after finishing your paper, or ask friends or loved ones to agree to cook dinner for you if you complete your project on time. Have them do the clean-up, too. You can do the same for them after they have accomplished a goal. Having a buddy hold you accountable can really help.
2. Do something to elevate your mood. Some comedy or good music often works.
3. Use if-then planning. "If I do this, then this will occur."
4. Remind yourself why what you are doing is important.
5. Take a 10-minute walk or have a little caffeine or sugar boost (these will only help in the short-term though).

Being busy but never really getting anything finished is stressful. It is not exactly a great motivator either. If this sounds like you, taking a closer look at your habits to see if you might be able to replace some of the counterproductive habits with better ones can help. Setting and accomplishing goals, no matter how small, will help you feel victorious and propel you forward. They motivate you. People like checking things off to-do lists. It feels good.

Seven Strategies for Motivating Yourself

Try the following seven strategies to regain your motivation and momentum. They really work.

1. **Have no more than three priorities for the day.**

   There are only so many things you can get done in a day and still enjoy it. Get into the habit of spending 5 minutes each night deciding what one thing you want to get done the next day. Ask yourself, "What would make me feel best about myself if I accomplished it?" Then do that thing first.

2. **Know the task before you start.**

   This is a must. When you do not do this, you can get lost in the millions of other activities that occupy your time, especially if tempted by the pull of the Internet or other interruptions. Assign yourself tasks to do (i.e. "respond to e-mails" or "take notes on Section I"). Assign times ("from 1 p.m. to 2 p.m."). Stop as soon as the end time arrives. You do not need to finish everything all at once.

3. **Put an end to activities that "leak."**

   Make a list of activities that can leak into your days. Stop the leaking by scheduling these activities (as opposed to letting them take over your day).

   For instance, instead of letting e-mail "leak" all over your day—all day every day—schedule e-mail as an activity at a certain time each day. Every activity should have a home—a space for its completion. Otherwise, you set yourself up for a full day of Attention Thievery.

4. **Take advantage of small slices of time.**

   It is easy to look up at the clock and see that you have 45 minutes before an appointment and think, "Well, I don't have time to do anything substantial. So, I guess I'll just watch the end of the news."

   Turn your thinking around. Learn to fit constructive things into small slices of time. Take notes on the first section of your reading assignment or write down a few brainstorming ideas for your upcoming paper or discussion piece. You might prefer to leverage these small chunks of time to address some of the daily tasks that need to get done each day like making your bed or prepping for dinner. It is amazing what you can complete in a short focused slice of time.

5. **Set an intention.**

   Before you begin any activity, set an intention for that activity. Do not worry if you feel silly doing this at first. It takes practice, but it works. Saying it out loud helps. Intend your desired outcome and imagine how you want to feel during the activity. This is the ultimate act of creativity and it helps motivate you to get things done.

6. **Toss out the things that do not nourish you.**

   Incoming e-mails, incessant text messages, group e-mails, magazine subscriptions, news feeds, Facebook updates, TiVo, underutilized memberships, unread books, etc. The list of incoming stuff goes on and on. It never ends. Until you choose to end it.

   Take stock of things. Get rid of anything that does not nourish you. If you subscribe to it, ask yourself why. Start letting go of stuff. Doing this one thing has helped countless students create a home and study/work environment that feels organized and healthy. Be ruthless about keeping the incoming stuff to a minimum.

7. **Be present in your downtime.**

   When you take a nap, take a nap. When you take an afternoon off, really take it off. Do not spend the day worrying about the things you should or could be doing. Do not bring the phone. Turn off the computer. Get out of the office. Do not clean the kitchen. Take a day for yourself. Fully disengaging from all of it from time to time to do something fun is imperative. Plus, this will allow you to return to your school, work, and loved ones with renewed energy and attention. Try it! Not only is it fun (once you get the hang of it), it really works.

Managing Stress

Stress is an epidemic nowadays. No matter where we turn, it seems like everyone is stressed out. We want to give back to our families, the communities we belong to, and so on. But there are only 24 hours in the day. Sometimes it feels like we will never catch up and no matter how hard we try, there will always be someone who is unhappy with what we give. All this pressure leads to stress. Lots and lots of stress. It is important to find ways to reduce the stressors in your life so you can focus on the good things: furthering your education, improving yourself and the world around you, and creating an even better future for yourself and your loved ones. All this is hard to do if you cannot find time for yourself or have difficulty using the time you do have.

One way to combat stress is to be sure you set aside time for yourself and your studies. Schedule it. Write it in your planner, calendar, or phone. The importance of this cannot be overstated. Here is why:

If you are like most students, you like to help others. But a compassionate desire to help others before yourself keeps many students stressed out and pressed for time. It also keeps you stuck in the same place year after year. If you have committed to going back to school to pursue your degree, we applaud you. It takes guts to enroll in an online program, and it also takes commitment to your studies and to yourself.

You may not be used to putting yourself and your needs first, but school is demanding and it is going to take you away from some of the things you used to do in your "free time." Many adults (especially parents) feel guilty when they prioritize their own education and dreams and start saying no to requests or demands that they no longer have time for. You do not have to feel that way. As you further your own education and dreams, you also inspire all those around you to do the same. Remember this blessing the next time you feel bad about having to say no to something or someone because you have to study or work.

Saying NO to Stress

Many of us are afraid to hurt other people's feelings by advocating for our needs and ourselves. So we give in, even though we know how much stress and trouble not being able to say no in the moment will create later on.

Here is the reason: When you go back to school and begin to change your life for the better, often the people closest to you struggle the most with these changes. They can sometimes undermine your progress without meaning to because change can be scary—and they like things as they are. If you have children or loved ones who might struggle with your decision to pursue your online program, take some time to talk honestly to them about what you need and how they can support you. Let them know that you are setting a good example, and ultimately, everyone benefits.

Online programs take just as much time, if not more, than traditional classes, so even though it may look like you are just sitting in front of the computer, they need to know you are "in class" and working hard to pursue your education. People who love you want to see you succeed. They are rooting for you (even if they want you to make dinner first).

Still, it is important to guard your dreams, goals, and time with care. When you start experiencing positive changes and hard-won successes in your life (academically, personally, professionally), you may discover that you end up saying no more than you are saying yes. This is often a good thing, and it will reduce your stress level.

Learning how to say no without guilt or explanation will drastically reduce the stressors and time and energy drains in your life. If you are going back to school and working, it is crucial you take the time you need for yourself. Go ahead and put yourself first for a change. Quote this book if you need back up. Highlight this section.

Give yourself this homework. Say no to that Friday night sleepover your kids want with their friends. Say no to making cookies for the bake sale. Say no watching your sister's kids on Saturday. Say no to filling in for the sick pianist when you should be studying. Say no helping your friend move on the one day you have off. Let your partner or roommate pick up the groceries and take the car in for an oil change. You will find you have much more to give when you learn to say no to things you really do not have the time or energy to do, and start saying yes to your own heart's desires and needs. It is a bold move, but this one tip alone can help assure your success.

You Are Not Alone

How Online Classmates Support One Another

One of the most important aspects of your online learning experience will be the collaboration with other members of the program to share experiences, complete group projects, and critique one another's work. Knowing how to communicate well and offer insightful feedback is key to supporting your colleagues and having them support you as well.

Developing an online social life and befriending your fellow classmates can really help keep you motivated throughout the term by offering additional opportunities to network and communicate with others about program content and additional questions you may have. While you will not be in the same physical space as your classmates, they are still integral to your online program.

Create a list of resources where you can access support and help when in a bind. Consider asking a classmate to be your accountability buddy. Try scheduling your time online in advance and "meeting" with your buddy in "real time" so you know when others will be in the same spot you are. And do not shy away from talking about your online courses with friends, family, and colleagues you are able to speak with face-to-face. Support from those in your immediate physical environment combined with the support, encouragement, and interactions you will have with your online peers and instructor will help you stay more connected to your program and your passion for what you do.

Family, Friends, and Colleagues

When we are not working, most of us spend the majority of our time at home. If the majority of your study and class time occurs when your family or roommates tend to be around, let them support you in the ways they can. Be sure to tell them your study schedule. It is a good idea to keep it posted in a common area like the refrigerator or a bulletin board. You could even have them add your "Do not disturb" times to their own schedules. It is easy to set a reminder on your phone or computer or synch your calendars so everyone is "on the same page."

Finding Helpful Resources

Contrary to what some people think, most online programs have the same resources available to them as traditional students in a brick-and-mortar classroom. It is simply untrue that there will be less available to you just because you are taking part in your education online. You should have access to everything traditional students do. This includes human resources such as librarians, counselors, and student support specialists (financial aid, academic planning, computer and tech issues, etc.). Programs and services are also available and encouraged for students with any sort of a disability or special need. There are accommodations that can (and must) be made if you have a disclosed and documented disability, including providing you with whatever necessary technology and support is required for you to participate fully in your online program.

In addition to basic resources, consider doing some research before beginning your online program to see what else might be available to you. Many programs offer a variety of internship or experiential options to supplement your online experience.

WorldCat, Online Catalogs, and America's Interlibrary Loan Program

Accessing books and other materials not readily available on the web or at your school or public library is easier than ever before. Almost all libraries have online catalogs that are easily accessible over the Internet or by visiting a local branch. In addition, everyone can freely use http://www.WorldCat.org to access or identify desired materials for school, work, or pleasure. This is an invaluable resource. If you do not know your way around http://www.Worldcat.org, free tutorials are available online.

Another option is the U.S. Interlibrary Loan program. Most Americans rarely take advantage of this gem (which has been available to library card holders since 1898). Through an Interlibrary Loan program, anyone with a library card can request to borrow books or other print media needed for research from all public libraries throughout the country. If your library does not have the book you are looking for, they can usually order it for you, even if the only library with the book is across the country. With a little time and patience, the country's resources are literally at your fingertips.

The Interlibrary Loan program is an underutilized but priceless option if the book or resource you need is not available locally or online.

Interlibrary Loan Tips

- Interlibrary loan policies vary from country to country and library to library.
- When requesting an item, you do not need to find a library that owns it. Librarians offer this as a service for you. If you want to research it yourself, however, the WorldCat website is the best place to look for items not owned by your local library.
- Many libraries have an online order form for interlibrary loan requests. If no online form is available, you will have to go in person to fill out a paper form.
- If an item is not available from libraries in your own country, it is possible, although often difficult, to get it from another country. When borrowing internationally, there may be charges for shipping and insurance. Check with your local interlibrary loan staff regarding questions on these charges and whether any costs will be passed on to you.
- A rare book may be hard to obtain, but some libraries are willing to lend books that may be considered rare. Rare items are almost always restricted to on-site use, meaning that the patron must use the book on library premises and will not be allowed to take it home. The alternatives are to look for a reprint or newer edition, search for the item at full-text or digitized book websites such as Project Gutenberg or Google Books™, and if necessary, pay to have a microfilm copy made.
- Journals are not usually loaned; rather, a photocopy is made of the needed article. Some sources charge a copyright fee, which may be anywhere from $2 to $40, and sometimes higher. Policies vary about whether these fees are passed on to the patron.
- New releases or high-demand titles are not always immediately available because most libraries need to satisfy local demand first. Similar limitations apply to textbooks.
- There is no set limit to the number of requests that can be submitted. However, your local library may not be able to process large numbers of transactions simultaneously from any one individual, depending upon

the library's staffing and resource levels. If you know you are going to need a large number of requests, you may need to schedule an appointment or meet with a subject specialist who can better help you with specific requests.

Do not be afraid to ask if you have any questions or concerns as you progress in your online program. Resources abound and are included in the price of your tuition so please use them.

Summary

Success in any online program depends on you. The tips, suggestions, and insights offered in this section and throughout this book can only work if you apply them to your individual situation and remain vigilant. By taking the initiative to understand your learning style, you are taking the first step toward success as an online student. Skills, such as reading comprehension, will be easier to approach if you have prepared a good study environment. Finally, manage your time wisely and stay organized.

Section II:
Getting Familiar With Technology

Please note that at the time of publication all Uniform Resource Locators (URLs) included in this text were current and operational. The purpose of this section is to provide general information on technology requirements and management for online learning. It is not meant to provide detailed instructions. Resources are provided for additional information.

Technology is a daily part of life for most of us. As an online student, technology is your school, your classroom, your library, and your file cabinet. Becoming comfortable with technology is key to your success. Technology requirements for your program include the hardware components, your computer, a monitor if you are using a desktop computer, a modem, speakers or a sound card, and a printer, plus software programs such as Adobe Acrobat®. (Please see the glossary at the end of this section for definitions.) Software programs required for online learning vary from institution to institution and from program to program. There are many moving parts to manage, but do not panic. Virtually all online institutions provide students with an information technology (IT) support team that students may contact when they encounter difficulties with the school's technology or need to troubleshoot issues with their computer, software, or Internet connection. Here are some guidelines and tips to get you started and keep you moving.

The Internet

Connecting to the Internet

You must be connected to the Internet to participate in an online program. Most people use an Internet service provider (ISP) to connect to the Internet through telephone lines (dial-up or digital subscriber line [DSL]), cable TV system, or satellite. Your ISP will most likely provide a modem and router for establishing a connection to your computer. The modem is connected to your computer and to a cable outlet (for cable broadband connections), or a phone jack (for DSL or dial-up connections). Cable, DSL, or other high-speed Internet options (except dial-up) are considered "always on," meaning that you do not need to perform extra steps to connect to the Internet every time you turn on your computer. Always-on connections can save you some time and trouble.

Navigating the Internet Using Browsers

A browser is what allows you to search on the Internet or "surf the web." Internet Explorer® was originally the most popular browser to surf the web, but now there are many from which to choose. The most popular browsers used in the United States are Internet Explorer (IE), Mozilla Firefox®, Safari®, and Google Chrome™. When you surf the web, you are connecting to web servers by either typing in an Internet address or URL, or clicking on a link. Web servers contain web pages. Your browser connects to the web server through its URL and requests a specific page, or if you do not request a specific page, it directs you to the web server's default page (the "home page").

Browser Expectations

You should have two of the following browsers installed on your computer, so you have a back-up in case one is not working properly:

- Internet Explorer (version 7.0 or higher)
- Google Chrome
- Mozilla Firefox
- Safari (for Mac®)

The browsers you use need to be Java™-enabled browsers. Java is a computer programming language that allows you to take full advantage of certain dynamic and interactive features of websites and the online classroom. If you do not have a Java-enabled browser, you can download and install the Java Virtual Machine for free online.

To be a responsible and safe Internet user, you should periodically check and make sure you have the latest version of the browser(s) you are using. Usually a pop-up reminder from the browser will let you know that a newer version is available and will ask you if you want to download it. To check which version of your browser you have installed, click on the Help option in the browser's toolbar and then select "About (the name of your browser)." The version number will be displayed. Newer versions of browsers usually help with "bugs" or other errors, and are generally safe and recommended.

The following resource can give you specific browser instructions for checking that Java is enabled and working on your computer: http://www.java.com. Use the search terms "testing" and "browser enable" to find up-to-date information.

Browsers—Maintaining Speed and Performance

Refreshing and checking your browser's cookies, cache (pronounced "cash"), and security settings at least once a week increases your browser's speed and performance. If a site you visit often does not load properly or displays old or outdated information, clearing out these items should solve the problem.

A cookie is a very small text file placed on a computer's hard drive by a web server to keep track of your session activity and to help your computer remember information about sites that you have visited in the past. For example, logging into the online classroom or your online banking website begins a session tracked by a cookie. If you are inactive for a certain amount of time (generally around a half-hour), your session will expire and you will have to log in again to continue your access. This is for your own safety and protection of your personal information.

The cache directory on your browser allows previously viewed websites to load much more quickly. For proper access to online classrooms and other websites, Internet security settings should be set to medium. When browser security is set too high, websites may be blocked or links may not work. While this is for your own protection, you will be unable to access many websites and online classrooms unless you lower your security settings. The following resources can offer specific browser instructions for checking your cache directory settings and clearing cookies:

- http://www.support.google.com
- http://www.bnl.gov/itd/webapps/browsercache.asp

Hyperlinks

Hyperlinks—usually blue underlined words or phrases—are a form of online navigation. Clicking on a hyperlink, or "link," takes you to another section in your course, another referenced website, an online document, or activity. Clicking a link may open a new browser window and display a document or a website. This content or data is considered a "download." Downloads also include e-mail that you receive and web pages you view, not just files that you download and actually save to your hard drive or external drive. Data that you send is an "upload."

Note for Windows® Users: If you do not close a window after you have finished reading it, and click back to your course window, the other window will remain open, although it may not be visible. If you click on another link, and it does not seem to open, the new link may have opened in the previously opened window. Thus, you will need to check your "Windows Document" bar at the very bottom of your computer screen and find the other browser window.

Clicking a link may open a new item in the main classroom viewing window instead of in a new browser window. If you are unable to figure out how to get back to the material you were viewing previously, simply click on the content item in the course navigation menu.

Bookmarking Sites

The web (and web browsers) evolve extremely quickly, but if there is one web browsing feature that has stood the test of time, it is browser bookmarks. Bookmarks on the Internet are just like bookmarks for printed books except that you are saving a link or URL for future reference instead of using a piece of paper to save your spot in the novel you are reading.

To bookmark in Internet Explorer: Go to the main menu under "Favorites." Select "Add to Favorites."

To go to your bookmarked web site in Internet Explorer: Go to the main menu under "Favorites." Select the title of the desired website.

To bookmark in Firefox or Netscape: Go to the main menu under Bookmark. Select "Bookmark This Page."

To go to your bookmarked website: Go to the main menu under "Bookmark." Select the title of the desired website. (If you do not see the title, select the "Go to Bookmarks" command. This will open a window of all your bookmarks. Search through this list for the title of the website. Select the title and then press the "Enter" key.)

Laptop Versus Desktop Ownership

Are you looking to buy a computer, but not sure if you want a desktop or a laptop? If you are beginning an online course, having your own computer is a huge advantage. It is important to weigh your options carefully because once you choose, you want to be happy with your choice. Sometimes knowing the disadvantages and advantages of having either a laptop or a desktop can help tremendously in the decision. Knowledge before the purchase is always a good thing.

It is a good idea to purchase the extra warranty for the computer. Many students fail to purchase it—and live to regret it. Repairs usually cost a lot more than the extra warranty price—something important to remember when in the market for a new computer.

PROS AND CONS

	PROS	CONS
Laptop	▪ Mobility ▪ Runs on a battery so can be used even when the power is out	▪ Cost—more expensive than a comparable desktop ▪ Size—laptop users often purchase larger monitors and keyboards
Desktop	▪ Cost—a desktop will usually cost you less money for the same or better components	▪ Lack of mobility

Working With Hardware and Software

In this section, we will discuss some tips for working with your hardware and software to keep your computer working smoothly and your files safe.

Hardware and Software Tips: Pop-up Blockers, Firewalls, and Antivirus and Anti-Spyware Programs

Pop-up Blockers

A pop-up is a type of window that appears on top of a browser window or website. While pop-ups can be disruptive in the form of online advertisements, you will need to allow them to see certain course resources. It is recommended that you set your browser to allow pop-up windows while accessing your classroom and the university's online resources. Most links, including course handouts and external links, open in a separate window, and they may not appear if pop-up windows are blocked. For questions related to pop-up blockers, refer to these resources and use the search terms "pop-up blockers" or "disable pop-up blockers."

- http://www.support.microsoft.com
- http://www.technipages.com/safari-enabledisable-pop-up-blocker.html
- http://support.google.com/chrome
- https://www.support.mozilla.org

Firewalls

It may help to think of firewalls as protecting you from "bad guys," whose job it is to break into your computer system. Your computer does not automatically recognize the bad guys. In order to be sure you can access the sites you visit often and know are safe (web-based e-mail, your school's website, etc.), you need to "tell" your computer they are safe. Once they are "inside," your computer will always presume they are one of the good guys.

Firewalls prevent people from accessing your computer or network without your knowledge or permission, and although they prevent a lot of potential security risks, they also often block access to many secure sites, such as e-mail, online classrooms, and online databases. Your firewall settings may need to be lowered or "turned down" in order to access secure sites. If you are having difficulty accessing a secure site or a particular link, check if you have a firewall system such as Norton™ or McAfee® installed on your system.

Keep in mind that it is smart to have a firewall if you have a broadband and/or wireless Internet connection because these connections are always on and broadcasting your computer's address. A computer's firewall system can be made up of personal firewall software, firewall hardware (such as a network router with firewall), or a combination of both. If you think you may have a firewall installed on your home computer, speak to the person who installed your computer, your ISP, or your computer manufacturer's customer care department to see how to modify the settings.

If you are at work or school, contact the IT department to determine if a firewall exists on your computer and what can be done to modify the settings. If you continue to have difficulty with access in your online classroom after adjusting your firewall settings, call your school's technical support team or your IT provider.

Viruses

Viruses can slow your computer's performance, cause your computer to crash, and damage files stored on your hard drive. More than 90% of all viruses are written for Windows-based computers.

Antivirus Software

Antivirus software scans your hard drive and other data storage devices (such as thumb drives) for viruses. Computers today are almost always sold with some form of virus protection installed. (Note that the virus protection that ships with a new computer often expires after a predetermined amount of time.)

How to Protect Yourself From Viruses

It is important to know how to keep your computer and your work protected from viruses. Although purchasing or downloading antivirus programs is the first step to protecting your computer, remember that it does not stop there. Regularly checking for software updates for your antivirus programs is essential. Many students just buy the antivirus software and never look at it again. This is a mistake. You need to actively keep your antivirus software up-to-date and functioning properly. Your laptop or desktop will likely remind you to update the software as needed, but it is a good idea to be proactive and check for updates every three months or so. Better safe than sorry is your mantra here.

In addition to regular antivirus software updates, the following tips will help avoid unwanted viruses from attacking your computer: Delete any and all suspicious-looking e-mails with attachments, even if the e-mail appears to be from a legitimate, known source, such as a friend or a fellow university student. If you have any doubt regarding whether an e-mail attachment is legitimate, send an e-mail to the person who appears to have sent the e-mail and confirm whether he or she actually sent it.

It is important not to open an attachment from someone you do not know. Opening an attachment can start the virus. Be suspicious of any e-mail without a subject in the subject line or that does not have the sender's name or e-mail address in plain view. Scan every file and attachment with your antivirus protection software before downloading or opening it.

Everyone should get virus protection for their computer. Scan your computer for viruses at least once a week, and update the virus definitions often. The importance of this cannot be overstated. Windows users should update their computer with the latest software from Microsoft Corporation to boost the security and reliability of their Windows personal computer (PC). For more information, go to Microsoft's home page (http://www.microsoft.com/) and check for the latest updates on a regular basis.

Three Ways to Check for Antivirus Software on Your Computer

If you have a new computer, odds are good that you will have antivirus software preinstalled on it. To know for sure, follow these steps:

1. Look for a shortcut on the desktop.
2. Check under the submenus in the Start menu.
3. Go to the Control Panel and open "Add/Remove Software" or "Programs and Features," depending on your operating system. This panel will show a listing of the software currently installed on your computer and should allow you to determine if virus protection has been installed.

Ensure that the program is running properly. If you need help with your particular antivirus software, look to the Help section or other documentation that came with the software.

Tips for Purchasing Antivirus Software

The following antivirus software products are generally acknowledged to be industry standards:

- McAfee Virus Scan
- Symantec/Norton™ Antivirus Software

You may want to check with your university's technical support before purchasing antivirus software. You can get updates for your antivirus software by visiting the software creator's website and following the directions to download virus signatures or definition updates. When purchasing antivirus software, consider purchasing the extended plan, in which updates are e-mailed to you. You may purchase these programs directly on the Internet and download the programs.

Free Antivirus Software

AVG Technologies Anti-Virus System (http://www.avg.com)

Note: This software may not have as many options or the support capabilities of commercial options.

Making Use of the University's Technical Support

Virtually all online institutions provide students with an IT support team that students may contact when they encounter difficulties with the school's technology, or when they need to troubleshoot issues with their computer, software, or Internet connection. In this section, we will take a look at how to best take advantage of your institution's technical support. Remember that your school's IT support team is a great resource if you need further assistance. Unfortunately, the university cannot assist you with any hardware problems you may encounter. One way to help Tech Support help you when you have a computer issue is to take a screenshot.

Screenshots

A screenshot is a picture you take of what you see on your computer screen. Your desktop is the first screen you see when your computer loads. If you call for technical assistance because you are having difficulty accessing or opening a specific website or document, you may be asked to send in a screenshot. This allows the person trying to assist you to see what you are seeing.

Try This: Practice taking a screenshot of your desktop by following these simple steps. For PCs, press the Print Screen (Prt Scrn, or Print Scrn) button located on the top right of your PC keyboard. (On some keyboards you may need to hold down the Control or function key and then Prt Scrn.) For Mac users, press Command + Shift + 3. Then, open a blank Word® document and paste the screenshot into the document. Do this by selecting Paste from the Edit menu bar or by pressing Control + V on a PC or Command + V on a Mac. Being able to take a screenshot of your desktop is a useful tool for both you and tech support to help them help you.

Working With Digital Media

Digital media refers to all types of digital content including text, video, audio, and graphics transmitted electronically on a computer using software, Internet, or computer networks. In this section, we will learn the value of the right-click, review how to highlight and select text, cut or copy and paste, and drag and drop selected text. We will end with a look at various media players available to students. You can move, edit, and manipulate digital text files. Here are few ways.

Highlight/Select Text

Highlighting or selecting text is usually the first step in a two-step action, followed by copy, cut, paste, or move. Highlighting is especially useful during word processing. You can highlight as little as a single letter or as much as an entire page. To highlight, using a traditional two-button mouse, left-click at the beginning of the text you want to highlight, hold the button down, and drag the mouse until all the desired text is highlighted. The text will remain selected even when you release the left mouse button. To remove the highlight from the text, left-click. If you have a new mouse without the "click" technique (mice are now available with new swipe technology), be sure to read the instructions and adapt these directions as needed.

Using a Right-Click

Right-clicking your mouse—pressing the right mouse button one time—almost always pops up a menu or list of actions relevant to the item or location on which you are clicking. To exit or close a right-click action, left-click once.

Right-clicking can also be used to access a file from a link on a website. Usually, you can open a file by left-clicking on the file's hyperlink (usually indicated by colored text that is underlined). If left-clicking on the hyperlink does not make the file open, you will need to right-click on the hyperlink.

Right-clicking on the hyperlink will cause a menu to appear that lists actions related to the hyperlink. If you wanted to save the file without opening it, move your cursor over Save Target As and left-click. If you wanted to look at the file first, move your cursor over Open and left-click.

For Mac users, holding the Control key while you click should bring up a similar menu of options.

Copy and Paste/Cut and Paste

Below are directions for how to copy and paste, and cut and paste. Note the first and third steps are the same for copy and paste, or cut and paste.

TABLE 3. COPY, CUT, AND PASTE

	COPY AND PASTE	CUT AND PASTE
1.	**Highlight the text you want to copy.**	
2.	**Copy the text.** Note: When you copy text you will not see anything happen (i.e., your screen will not change). You can copy using any of these methods: ■ Toolbar Menus: Left-click on Edit in the toolbar at the top of your Word screen, then select Copy from the menu. ■ Keystrokes: Press the Control (Ctrl) key; hold down the Ctrl key while you press the C key. ■ Right-click Menus: Right-click; select Copy from the menu.	**Cut the text.** You can cut using any of these methods: ■ Toolbar Menus: Left-click on Edit in the toolbar at the top of your Word screen, then select Cut from the menu. ■ Keystrokes: Press the Control (Ctrl) key; hold down the Ctrl key while you press the X key. ■ Right-click Menus: Right-click; select Cut from the menu.
3.	**Place your cursor where you want to paste the text.** Note: The paste function will be unavailable unless you have copied or cut text. You can paste using any of these methods: ■ Toolbar Menus: Left-click on Edit in the toolbar at the top of your Word screen, then select Paste from the menu. ■ Keystrokes: Press the Control (Ctrl) key; hold down the Ctrl key and press the V key. ■ Right-click Menus: Right click; select Paste from the menu.	

Drag and Drop

Drag and drop is commonly used to move an item, such as a file or text, from one location to another (i.e., an item is "dragged" from its old location and "dropped" into a new location). For example, a user might drag and drop a file from one folder into another folder.

There are only three steps to dragging and dropping something:

1. Highlight the text, or press and hold down the left mouse button while the cursor is over an object.
2. Continue to hold down the button while moving the cursor to a different location.
3. Release the mouse button.

Media Players

Video and audio media are used extensively in online programs. Most institutions provide some type of media player for students to use to access this content. A media player delivers media content, including video and audio, through streaming media channels or through downloads direct to your computer or mobile media device, such as a compatible cell phone. Typically, if a course contains media, you will see the media player listed on the learning resources page. There are a wide variety of media players used by institutions. It is best to contact your specific institution for instructions or questions on how to use or troubleshoot your media player.

Managing Your Files

You will generate a lot of work in your online program. This translates to creating and keeping track of a large number of files. In this section, we will take a closer look at the importance of file folders and using best practices for naming and saving your files. We will also look at how to back up your work, how to save various types of files, what to do when you cannot open attachments, and what to do if or when the Internet is down. Through all the tangles of online work, it is important to remember to anticipate and prepare for problems.

Developing a system beforehand that works for you and keeps things organized is important. Creating the right system for your computer files will save you from a lot of headaches later. There are different schools of thought on managing your files, but a simple way to get started is just to create a new folder for each program or class. Within that folder you may want to create subfolders to store files for various assignments or chapters and sections. If you are a visual person and being able to "see" your folders or work reassures you, you can create the folders right on your desktop. That way every time you start up your computer you can rest assured all program files are right there.

The Importance of File Folders

As you progress in your program, you should consider creating a master folder to store your work from each quarter or semester. Being able to store the folders from programs taken each semester, quarter, or year will help you keep track of them without feeling like your computer is being taken over by folders. No matter how you decide to organize and systematize your work, it is a good idea to create the system and folder structure at the beginning of each semester or quarter. Not only does it reassure you that things will be organized, it will make it quicker and easier for you to figure out where to save your work.

Pay close attention to where your files are saved by default. While you can change the location where files are downloaded or saved, many computers automatically save files to My Documents. Though some students prefer saving documents to the desktop or C drive, it is important to remember to keep the location consistent and back up and save files not only from My Documents, but from your desktop and entire C drive as well. The old adage, "better safe than sorry" applies here.

Naming and Saving Work: How to Name Your Files

Though it sounds simple enough, figuring out how to name your files and keep track of your work requires forethought. Again, developing a system that works for you will help you stay organized and on track. When you establish and adhere to a file-naming system early on, you set yourself up for success by lessening the odds of losing files, sharing or turning in the wrong files or file types, and possibly losing points for not following directions.

The Importance of File Extensions

When opening files from your instructor or peers, the file extension type (the automatically generated information provided after the period in the file name) should provide you with valuable information. This "code" of sorts lets you know whether or not you have the proper software on your computer for opening the file. Common file extensions are: .doc (Microsoft Word document), .docx (Office® 2000 document), .pdf (portable document file, usually via Adobe Acrobat), .ppt (PowerPoint slideshow presentation), .mov (video file), .jpg (image/photo), and .wav (audio file). These are only some of the common file extensions you will come across in your online program.

Instructor Tip for File Naming

Before using your "go-to" file name-saving system, you should always first check your syllabus for the file naming convention to be used in the program, if specified. Different instructors may have different preferences or requirements for file naming and sharing. Furthermore, it is important to check individual assignment directions; you may be asked to use a specific file name for that assignment. Be sure to double-check your file name before sending any files.

While often overlooked, the file extension is an important part of the file name. Do not, under any circumstances, change the file extension type. For example, do not change a .doc to a .docx file yourself. Having the proper extension in the file name is very important when managing your files. This part of the file name is automatically added and should not be changed. Doing so may render your file invalid. This is because without the correct file extension (for example, using a .docx extension instead of a .ppt extension for a PowerPoint presentation), your computer will be unable to automatically open the file using the correct application.

But do not worry—virtually all computer software programs (such as Microsoft Word or Adobe Acrobat) will automatically generate the correct file extension for your file without you having to do a thing. Just remember, if you do not change this automatically generated file extension, you should have no troubles.

Best Practices for Naming Files

In general, the following best practices should be followed when naming your files. These are guidelines only.

- Do not include any of the following special characters in your file name; they can prevent your instructor or fellow students from opening the file: % ~ = / \ : * ? " < > | #) ' $
- Do not leave any blank spaces. Use an underscore instead of a blank.
- Include your last name and first initial.

- Include the week or module number.
- Include the assignment title (or a shortened version of it). This is one possible example: Jess Jones would name a Week 3 assignment titled "Goals" as follows: "Jones_J_w03_goals.doc"

When naming files and including dates, it is important to place a zero in front of single numbers so the files sort in actual numeric order in your file list (for example, February 5th 2012 would be named as 02_05_12 rather than 2_5_12). If you fail to do this, files for weeks 10-12 appear before files for week one, which only creates unnecessary confusion.

What to Do When File Attachments Cannot Be Opened

Even if you are sure you saved your file correctly, sometimes an assignment or file you send or upload as an attachment cannot be opened by your instructor or peers. While it may be that the recipient does not have the correct software to open the file, oftentimes an erroneous character in a file name can prevent a Word document from opening. Remember, do not use any of these characters when naming a Word file: % ~ = / \ : * ? " < > | #) ' $. If you have the latest version of Office, remember that your instructor may be using an older version. Resave your document, making sure you change the "Save as Type" Word 97-2003 or 6.0/95-RTF (*.doc).

Note to Office 2007 and Earlier Users: If you receive a .docx, .pptx, .ppsx, or .xlsx file and cannot open it with your version of Office, ask the sender to resave the file. In the "Save As..." option, select "Word/Excel®/PowerPoint 97-2003 Document." Then, download and install the free upgrade mentioned above.

Best Practices for Saving Files

When it comes to saving files, it is always better to err on the side of caution. Therefore, it is important to save files early, and save them often. It is a good idea to save all work, assignments, and discussion postings to your computer's hard drive, and to CDs or an external drive, such as a thumb drive. This is important because all computers—even new ones—can "crash" without warning. Files saved only on your hard drive will be lost forever. Files backed up on an external device or drive can be retrieved even after a computer "crashes." *Note:* Typically, online programs cannot retrieve work from your online classroom once the program has ended—therefore, you MUST save all of your work to an external source to protect it in the case of a system crash.

How to Save Word-Processed Documents

1. Go to the navigation menu and select File, then Save As. A Save As box will appear.
2. Determine where you want the document to be saved (e.g., My Documents, desktop, an external drive). Make sure this location is in the Save In box. If you want to save your file to an external drive or disc, pull down the drop-down menu and select a location. Look for External Drive and the drive letter associated with it. For this assignment, select Desktop.
3. Type the name of the file in the File Name box.
4. Microsoft Word defaults to Word Document *.doc in the Save As Type box.
5. Click on Save. Your document should now appear on your desktop.
   Note About Windows Office 2007: Microsoft Office 2007 saves files in formats that are different from previous versions of Office: .docx, .pptx, .ppsx, and .xlsx. If you have older versions of Microsoft Office, you cannot access Office 2007 files unless you download and install a free upgrade. The upgrade will allow you to open, edit, create, and/or save the new file types (.docx, .pptx, .ppsx, or .xlsx) To download and install a free upgrade, "Microsoft Office Compatibility Pack for Word, Excel, and PowerPoint 2007 File Formats," go to the following website: http://www.microsoft.com/

Two Ways to Save Linked Documents

1. Click on a document link.
2. The document will open in a new window.
3. Select File from the menu bar of the new window that contains the chosen document.
4. Select Save As.
5. The file name of the document should already be filled in. Choose the location where you want to save your file and then click on Save.

Right-Click on the Document Link

1. Right-click on the document link.
2. From the menu that appears, select Save Target As.
3. The filename of the document should already be filled in.
4. Choose the location where you want to save your file and then click on Save.

How to Track Changes in Microsoft Word

Your instructor may grade your assignments using Microsoft Track Changes. This allows your instructor to insert comments into your paper and to add and remove words, sentences, or paragraphs. When you get an assignment back from your instructor, be sure to turn on Track Changes under the Review pane so that you can see feedback and suggestions from the instructor in addition to your grade. If you look at your document and cannot see any comments, remember that the Track Changes feature must be "turned on."

In Word 2007 and later, click on the Review tab, then click on Track Changes. A drop-down menu will open; select Track Changes. For more information on using Track Changes in Word, refer to the following resource: http://www.office.microsoft.com.

Backing up Your Work

The importance of "backing up" your work cannot be overstated. When you back-up your files at least on a weekly basis, you can rest assured that all of your hard work will not be lost if your system crashes, the hard drive freezes, or your computer somehow loses its data. Though these unfortunate events are less common with today's technological advancements, it still happens. Mistakes get made. Laptops get dropped and all computers get spilled on regularly. Be sure to take a few moments each week to back up your program files to a secondary (external) hard drive, a thumb drive, or another data storing device such as a recordable CD/DVD or copy files onto a shared server. Many institutions these days offer free storage on their servers for students and staff. It is highly recommended that you take advantage of such storage solutions if available. It is often as simple as performing a "File Save As" and saving your work to your computer and another outside location as well. This can be done at the time of the original save or later on (once weekly is advised).

What to Do if the Internet Is Down

Technology is far from perfect. Systems fail. Servers go offline. Interruptions in our online technologies happen. It sometimes seems like the system crashes or the Internet goes down when you need these things the most: when an assignment is due by midnight or when you must complete an online assessment by tomorrow morning and only have a few hours in the evening to take the test. To avoid being blindsided by technology failures, it is best to anticipate in advance what you would do if the Internet were down or the system crashed. Much like you need to have a fire escape plan just in case the hamburger burns more than the pan, you will want to have an "Oh no, the Internet is down" escape plan, as well.

When creating your contingency plan, be sure you know how and where to locate and utilize an additional computer with Internet access in case your connection stops working for some reason. Ask at the local library or even a nearby school or community center and see if and how they would be able to help you in the event of a crash. You should also find a "buddy" in your program who you can call or somehow contact if the Internet is down. While you may be able to e-mail or text message from your phone, it is always a good idea to exchange phone numbers, as well. That way you know you have at least one "buddy" in your class to give you updates and information (besides the instructor, who may be less than pleased to receive a late night call from a procrastinating student who just lost his or her Internet connection). You should also have and offer your "buddy" and instructor an alternate e-mail account in case your primary or school e-mail goes down or is temporarily unavailable. Lastly, be sure to have the contact information of your buddy and instructor handy as well as the IT support number. Then, take a deep breath and relax, knowing you will be all right no matter what obstacles modern technology throws your way.

Online Education Management Systems: Web Portals, E-mailing, Texting, Chat and Discussion Boards, Blogs

While it can be overwhelming to prepare for all the things an online student needs to know, it is important to understand the intricacies of your online education management system's components before you begin your program. In this section we will take a closer look at web portals, online chat and discussion boards, and how to navigate and use blog, vlogs, instant-messaging, and e-mail with proper skills and etiquette.

Web Portals, Chat, and Discussion Boards

Many online institutions have a web portal or student portal home page that serves as the main starting place (usually a personalized home page) where students in online programs log on to access their courses and information. There will be a menu of options to choose from that will direct you to the proper place (grades, e-mail, syllabus, assignments, discussion board posts, class blog, etc.). Various online course management systems exist and vary from school to school. Popular online course management systems include Blackboard Inc. and Moodle (your school may use a different name) and usually allow students to access all course materials; find assignments, updated grades, and comments; visit and respond in live chat rooms; post on discussion boards; and e-mail or contact classmates and the instructor directly from the online course management system.

If all this sounds like a foreign language to you, do not worry. Your school and instructors will offer a training and support system going over the features of the system and what programs are required for the course. Usually the orientation or training is done online, but there may be an in-person option as well. Many schools also offer virtual round-the-clock help to students who need IT or computer support.

Texting, Chatting, and Messaging

A text message is a typed message sent through your phone (short message service [SMS]), often made up of abbreviated words or phrases. A "chat" in an online context refers to typing messages on a computer network to someone. It requires an Internet connection and involves typing brief messages back and forth and waiting for the person on the other end to respond. Real time "chatting" can be useful in online programs when you need a question addressed quickly.

Instant messaging is free, but should also be used only if you have received permission to instant message (IM) with the person beforehand. An instant message is a private text-based "live" conversation that takes place between two people who are communicating over the Internet at the same time. You can also "IM" someone photos and other files in addition to text, depending on the instant messaging system or chatroom.

It helps to know some of the terminology involved with many chats, messages, and texts. It really is like learning a new language sometimes: LOL (laughing out loud), ROFL (Rolling on the floor laughing), BRB (be right back), OMG (Oh my gosh!), IKR (I know, right?), etc. While texting is never required in online programs, it may be used as a means of communication. Make sure you have permission to text someone before doing so. E-mailing them first is usually recommended because some people incur a charge for each text message sent or received. This can quickly add up, and the recipient sometimes has no choice in the matter.

All these tools come with their own etiquette and quirks. The general rule, though, is if you are unsure if you should text or chat or "IM" with someone, do not. Take the time to ask him or her about it first and avoid boundary issues that may arise as a result of contacting someone without permission first.

Blogs and Vlogs

A blog is a "web log" or website usually containing journal-type entries by a "blogger" or writer. Some blogs have multiple bloggers and readers of the blog are usually able to leave comments on individual blog posts (unless comments are disabled for that particular post). To leave a comment, you may have to give a name, set up an account, type a brief phrase, or provide some contact information so the blogger knows you are not a spammer (someone who sends unsolicited e-mail). Information on how to leave a comment is usually provided on the blog.

With the advent and increasing popularity of YouTube™, vlogs are quickly replacing the popularity of blogs. A vlog is a "video blog," where the owner/author of the website or blog uploads videos or videotaped messages to watch instead of typing out a written blog message, though there may be accompanying text. Many computers and smart phones have built in camcorders and cameras thereby making it quite easy to record a video message for others. Your program may require you to contribute to a blog or vlog, but rest assured that courses requiring use of such skills will provide you with a tutorial or other support prior to the assignment due date.

E-mailing

Today e-mail is virtually unavoidable, especially in an online program. Though many of us use e-mail regularly, it cannot hurt to brush up on your technical skills and refresh your knowledge of how to best use many of the valuable features e-mail provides (and avoid the common pitfalls as well). It is important to know what kind of e-mail you will need to use: your school e-mail or your personal e-mail (usually a web-based e-mail, such as Gmail™, Hotmail®, Yahoo!® mail, or an e-mail software program). Most instructors and institutions will insist you check and use your school e-mail only for school work. Be sure to know what is and is not acceptable in each program, and remember that the institution is usually responsible for maintenance and troubleshooting on your school account only. There is no guarantee that your IT support team can or will help you with personal e-mail issues, though it does not hurt to ask.

Tips for E-mailing

- **Know how attachments work.** You will likely have to send an e-mail attachment at some point in your program. Practice attaching files via e-mail before your program begins, and make sure you know the file size limit on your e-mail account and the recipient's prior to sending, or larger files may be returned.
- **Use a smart phone as back-up, if possible.** Keep in mind that e-mail only works when you are connected to the Internet. If your modem or home networking is down, it may be possible to check, send, and receive e-mail from a smart phone with 3 or 4G technology, or a portable Hot Spot connection on the phone (additional charges for such features apply).
- **Be mindful of your signature and remove the quotes and stationery.** Most e-mail programs offer you the opportunity to create a signature that is included at the end of every e-mail. Your signature should be appropriate, be short, and provide essential information for contacting you in reply to e-mail messages. Most companies and schools discourage students and faculty/staff from using inspirational quotes and personalized stationery on their work or school e-mail. If you insist on using a quote, joke, or opinion, make sure these are not too long or potentially offensive, especially if using your school e-mail account. If you not available via e-mail for a period of time, including this in the signature or creating an out-of-office message is a good idea.
- **Keep e-mails organized and up-to-date.** Much like you would create folders for your program files and assignments, you will want to stay organized and on top of your e-mail inbox. It is not a good idea to store all of your e-mails in your inbox or to wait too long between checking e-mails. If you are not on e-mail often, let folks know you only check once or twice daily, so they are not expecting an instant reply message. It is a good idea to have e-mail folders for each program you enroll in, and you can create filters to automatically not only send your messages to your inbox, but house them in distinct folders as well. Check with your e-mail provider for specific directions on how to do this, as e-mail software and systems vary.

A Note on Smart Phone Apps

Applications (apps) are software programs that run on your smart phone, such as a BlackBerry®, iPhone®, or Android™. Many of these apps are free to download onto your phone (or iPad® or iPod®), and those that do cost money are generally quite inexpensive. There are myriad tools that can help you stay organized and on task, and many schools and institutions nowadays have their own downloadable apps for students and staff. If you are prone to using your smart phone more than your computer, taking the time to research, download, and figure out how to best use some of these apps could really help with your educational success.

Summary

As an online student, it is so important to get comfortable using technology, including understanding your computer and its components, how to use software programs such as Adobe Acrobat and Microsoft, and how to navigate the Internet. Remember that virtually all online institutions provide students with an IT support team that students may contact when they encounter difficulties with their computer or the school's online management system.

Glossary of Technical Terms

Online learners need to be familiar and comfortable with using technical terms. Knowing and using technical words will make it easier for you to communicate with your instructor, colleagues, and technical support.

Address Bar: The field at the top of a web browser where you enter the URL for the website you want to view. For example, if you want to visit Yahoo!, Inc.'s main site, you would type http://www.yahoo.com in the address bar.
Attachment: A file sent with an e-mail. Almost any file type can be sent as an attachment (Word documents, image files, spreadsheets, etc.), and it is possible to attach multiple files to the same e-mail.
Browser: A software application that allows you to access Internet content. Internet Explorer, Firefox, and Safari are all examples of browsers.
Cache: (pronounced "cash") A location on your computer where files are stored temporarily for quick access. When you visit a web page, the page

is stored in the cache directory on your hard drive. If you want to return to the page later, the browser can retrieve it from the cache rather than from the page's server. This saves you time and lessens the burden of additional traffic on the network. To increase speed and ensure you have the most up-to-date version of the websites you are visiting, it is helpful to empty your stored browser cache on a regular basis.

Cookie: A special text file that a website puts on your hard drive so that it can remember something about you at a later time. A cookie records your preferences when using a particular site. For your online courses, cookies are used to handle your user ID and password information whenever you log in to the site. The online classroom uses cookies to ensure the privacy of your account when you enter secure parts of the site. A cookie set by your online classroom may remember your username and password for later visits and allow you to participate in your classes in a way that is as efficient and easy as possible. As with the cache, it is helpful to empty your stored browser cookies when a website is not loading properly or you have recently changed your log-in information.

Desktop: The main screen of the Windows and Mac operating system. After you have logged in to your computer, the desktop is the first screen you see. The desktop displays icons, which are small picture representations of programs or files.

Digital Media: Digital media refers to all types of digital content including text, video, audio, and graphics transmitted electronically on a computer using software, Internet, or computer networks. The most common types of digital media are text documents and files.

Firewall: A set of related programs designed to prevent unauthorized access to a computer or computer network through an Internet connection. Many companies set up a firewall so employees cannot do certain things on the Internet, such as chat. A firewall can also prevent people who do not work at your company from accessing the company's private data resources.

Hard Drive: (also referred to as a "hard disk drive") It is usually the main storage device of your computer. It holds the operating system and any programs that have been installed on the computer. You can save your work to the hard drive (usually designated as the "C" drive). Today's computers typically come with a hard drive that will hold hundreds of gigabytes of data.

Hardware: The physical components of computers and related devices. The monitor, modem, and keyboard, as well as the computer itself, are all examples of hardware.

Hyperlink: A connection between one document or web page and another or between sections within a document or website. Clicking on a "link" takes you to the new location. Text, images, and areas of a page can all be turned into hyperlinks. The most common form of a link is a highlighted or underlined word or picture that can be clicked by the user.

Internet: The Internet (sometimes called simply "the Net") is a worldwide system of computer networks in which any one computer can, if it has permission, get information from any other computer (and sometimes talk directly to users at other computers). The Internet is a public, cooperative, and self-sustaining facility that is available to millions of people worldwide. While commonly confused, the Internet is not the same as the World Wide Web. The web is part of the Internet.

Internet Service Provider (ISP): A business that provides access to the Internet. An ISP is a service you normally pay for, similar to service with a phone company. An ISP may also give you an e-mail account. Examples of ISPs include Verizon, Charter Communications Holding Company, LLC, and BellSouth Corporation®.

Log in: The process of entering identifying information into a computer program to gain access. When you log in to your course, your computer is connecting to the computer where your institution's online data is stored. (The one-word term "login" is often used to mean a person's user ID.)

Modem: A device that allows you to connect to the Internet through an analog phone line, like the one most people have in their homes.

Random Access Memory (RAM): The place in a computer where the operating system, application programs, and data in current use are kept so that they can be quickly reached by the computer's processor. RAM can be compared to a person's short-term memory, while the computer's hard drive can be compared to the long-term memory. Unlike the hard drive, which can become completely full of data so that it will not accept any more, RAM will never run out of memory. It keeps operating, but can become very slow if overloaded. Rebooting your computer clears RAM.

Scroll Bar: A graphical object that allows you to drag hidden portions of a screen into view. Some pages in your course will be too long or wide for you to view on your screen. You will find an area at the side or bottom of the screen that will allow you to move up and down or side-to-side on the page. Click on either arrow at the top/bottom or left/right of the scroll area, or click and drag the bar to view the page.

Server: A computer that shares resources with client computers or links together computers in a network. Websites are stored on servers, and most businesses use one or more servers to keep employees connected.

Software: A general term for the various kinds of programs used to operate computers and related devices. Microsoft Word is an example of software. Some software is free.

Thumb Drive: (also called an external drive or jump drive) A portable storage device that can be connected to a computer via a USB port. To use a thumb drive, insert it into a USB port on your computer. To access the thumb drive, navigate to My Computer or Computer, then select the device. You can now access files on the drive or save files to the drive.

Uniform Resource Locator (URL): A website's address. Every website has a unique URL.

Vlog: A "video blog," where the owner/author of the website or blog uploads videos or videotaped messages to watch instead of typing out a written blog message, though there may be accompanying text.

World Wide Web: (also referred to as the web or WWW) A system for accessing information over the Internet. All of the different resources that people have made available through online servers form a giant web of information that can be accessed through web browsers. The web has been described as "the universe of network-accessible information, an embodiment of human knowledge." (retrieved from http://searchcrm.techtarget.com/definition/World-Wide-Web)

Website: One or more pages written in hypertext markup language (HTML) and stored on a web-accessible server that can be accessed through a unique URL. A website may contain text, images, video, audio, and interactive components. The first page of a website is referred to as the site's "home page." All websites combine to form the World Wide Web.

Section III: Completing Coursework and Following Course Requirements

The beginning of class can be an exciting but stressful time for students. Once you are ready for your class to begin, your mind may drift toward questions about what will be required of you and when your assignments are due. You hope your questions will be answered in a clear and straightforward manner so you are not left wondering what to do, how to do it, and when. This is the power of the syllabus.

Understanding the Syllabus

What exactly are you and other students supposed to do with a class syllabus? The short answer is everything. But let us first take a look at the purpose of a syllabus before moving on. The syllabus serves several functions. Think of the syllabus as both your compass (telling you which direction you are heading) and roadmap (providing specific directions for how to reach the end destination) for your course. While specifics that appear on a syllabus may vary (depending on the instructor and the course), in most cases the syllabus will include the below information:

- The name, contact information, office location, office hours, and preferred meeting methods for the instructor.
- Course title and section number, time and dates of class, description of the class, and the specific learning objectives. Learning objectives outline the skills, tasks, and knowledge you will be taught and expected to demonstrate by the end of class.
- Class rules or guidelines and the instructor's expectations of students.
- Information about the class materials: textbook(s), articles, or any other assigned readings.
- Dates of tests, quizzes, projects, presentations, assignments, and readings/discussions. Often the instructor will also include details, such as instructions and descriptions of outlined materials.

- An outline and/or calendar showing the topic(s) covered during each class meeting.
- Class policies, assessment, and grading scales or rubrics for assignments and formal assessments (tests/quizzes/projects).

Syllabi Length

A word of caution on syllabi length: Do not confuse the length of a syllabus with the difficulty of the class or use syllabus length as a measure of the projected workload.

This is your opportunity to understand what you can expect to get out of the class, decide whether these objectives meet your needs, and know what you will need to do to meet the objectives.

Know the Course Calendar

Prepare for each class by looking at the syllabus. New college students often misunderstand due dates. Any reading or other assignments associated with a specific day on the syllabus' calendar must be prepared by class time that day or by the assignment due date.

Understanding Class Policies

Some policies listed on the syllabus are college- or institution-wide policies. Instructors are usually required to include these on their syllabi, but it is important to clarify any discrepancies and address unanswered questions with your instructor.

It is a good idea to read the student publications, as it is your responsibility to know what is expected of you, regardless of whether or not it is in the syllabus. A typical example is the policy on academic honesty, also referred to as academic integrity (cheating and plagiarism). Other policies are more idiosyncratic, meaning they are unique to the particular instructor and course. Wise students pay attention to such policies because they provide clues as to what is important to your instructor. This may include, but is not limited to, policies on attendance, tardiness, excused absences, grading, late work, participation, cell phones, and other distractions.

If you like being on your instructor's good side, you definitely should make time to read those policies carefully and follow them closely. Remember that if extra credit is not specified, it is likely not allowed. So do not expect to turn all your work in at the last minute and turn in extra credit assignments to help boost your grade. Extra credit is rare. In addition, it is important to take special note of the class grading policy, which may or may not be college-wide. Know how many points or what percentage equals each grade, whether late work is accepted, and the penalty for turning work in after the deadline. Submitting work late can make or break your grade.

Rubrics for Grading and Assessment

Have you heard of rubrics? Rubrics are tools that help you and your instructor assess your work and assign a grade on a particular project, paper, or assignment. Not all rubrics look or function the same, and some may even seem very complex and confusing. Generally, a rubric presents categories that make up the critical components of an assignment, such as understanding specific course content, incorporating supporting evidence, and using basic writing skills. The components may be presented along a scale, with examples for inadequate, adequate, or exemplary work.

Think of a rubric as a tool that helps you understand what is required to earn points on an assignment rather than as a tool for penalization. Use rubrics as a way to check your work before submitting it. Ask yourself, "Have I done everything indicated in the rubric to earn the maximum points?" Below are two sample rubrics; the first provides you with a rubric for a writing assignment, the second with a participation rubric that establishes an overall level and grade based on the demonstrated level of proficiency. These sample rubrics provide you with two possible rubric styles you may encounter throughout your academic career.

Rubric 1

TABLE 4. SAMPLE RUBRIC 1 FOR WRITING ASSIGNMENT

CRITERIA	NOT PROFICIENT	PROFICIENT	HIGHLY PROFICIENT
Thesis Statement (Originality and Clarity)	Thesis is missing or too obvious; reader cannot determine an original thesis—or thesis is unrelated to the assignment.	Thesis is obvious or unimaginative in nature; purpose of thesis vague or loosely related to the assignment.	Clear thesis that demonstrates fresh insights that challenge the reader's thinking.
Organization and Flow	Paper lacks focus and employs little or no transitions; abrupt or illogical shifts and confusing or ineffectual flow of ideas.	Paper's organization supports the thesis and flows logically from point to point; employs appropriate transitions and sequencing of ideas throughout.	Paper's flow and organization are easy to follow and fully supportive of thesis and purpose; effective and clear transitions and sequencing of ideas.
Supporting Ideas/Details and Reasoning	Support too generic and ideas too broad or irrelevant to thesis; displays undeveloped or unoriginal support and reasoning; repetitive.	Appropriate use of examples and details to support thesis; solid reasoning is evident; employs original ideas and avoids assumptions.	Concrete development of ideas; all assumptions are made explicit; details provided are original, germane, and convincingly interpreted.
Sources and Documentation	Source material is used erroneously (plagiarism and/or improper paraphrasing and quotations); sources inconsistently referenced throughout paper.	Properly and consistently uses sources to extend ideas and inform, but occasionally fails to conform perfectly to required style manual specifications (Modern Language Association [MLA], American Psychological Association [APA], Chicago Style).	Seamless use of sources from a variety of quality sources to support, extend, and inform the reader without substituting the writer's own development of ideas; proper use of quotes, paraphrasing, etc.

Sample Rubric 2 for Course Participation (Beginner—Advanced)

Participation is a matter of active engagement demonstrated by working effectively within your groups and displaying consistent cooperation and respect for others. The quality of your participation in this course will be evaluated according to the four levels below:

Level 1 Participation (Beginner—"D" Grade)

- Little or no advance preparation
- Lets others set and pursue the agenda
- Observes passively and says little or nothing
- Responds to questions
- Gives the impression of wanting to be somewhere else
- Attendance record is haphazard and inconsistent; may be absent or late without notice

Level 2 Participation (Novice—"C" Grade)

- Occasionally or partially prepared in advance
- Takes on a limited role in setting group goals and agendas
- Tends to prefer that others provide the direction of group discussions
- Occasionally but unreliably introduces information or asks questions
- If likely to be absent or late, informs others ahead of time and arranges to cover own responsibilities

Level 3 Participation (Proficient—"B" Grade)

- Consistently well prepared in advance
- Takes a large part in setting group goals and agendas
- Actively participates in discussion and asks or answers questions regularly
- Regularly listens actively and shows understanding by paraphrasing or by acknowledging and building on others' ideas
- Volunteers willingly and often; consistently carries own share of the group's responsibilities

Level 4 Participation (Advanced—"A" Grade)

All of the markers of proficient participation, plus:

- Regularly draws out ideas or concerns of others, especially those who have written or said little
- Consistently revisits issues or ideas that need more attention
- Repeatedly helps the group stay on track
- Summarizes group decisions, actions, and assignments

A Few Final Words on Syllabi

One policy your instructor may include on the syllabus is a disclaimer that the syllabus is subject to change. While neither students nor instructors like syllabus changes, they are occasionally necessary. Be prepared for changes, and be sure you understand them well. Ask questions or meet with your instructor if the changes are unclear.

Instructors may offer the syllabus solely online. You can, of course, print out this online document, but also bookmark it and consider adding it to your "favorites." You should be in the habit of checking it online regularly. Unlike in high school, you will not get frequent reminders about test dates, quiz dates, and assignment and project due dates in college. You are expected to know these due dates. Thus, the syllabus is critically important for keeping on top of what is due and when.

To avoid undue stress and conflicts, at the beginning of the semester it is always a good idea to compare syllabi for all your classes and while you are entering due dates into your time-management system (refer back to Section II for further tips). If you notice overwhelming conflicts in due dates among your classes, you may want to consider dropping a class or otherwise rearranging your schedule. You can also talk to your instructors to see if, together, you can find ways around potential major conflicts. Above all, be sure to communicate any questions or concerns right away. Do not wait until the end of the class to contact the instructor and expect optimal results. The time to contact the instructor is the moment you are confused or get the first bad grade. Do not be intimidated by your instructors (regardless of how many letters they have behind their names). They are teaching for a reason, so do summon the courage and contact them and get the information you need to succeed. Do not fret if you do not immediately receive an e-mail or call back from your instructor. Like you, instructors are busy and may need a day or two to respond. The time you can expect to wait for a response varies from instructor to instructor and course to course. Consult your syllabus or simply ask if unsure of the parameters. You will certainly be glad you did, and your instructor will appreciate it, too.

Reporting Technical Problems

It is a good idea to contact the instructor right away if you notice a problem with the course; for example, if you find a broken link. Odds are good that the instructor will appreciate knowing right away that there is an issue, even prior to the start of class. Doing so ensures accuracy of information and assures students everything is in working order by the first day of class.

Communicating concerns and questions that arise after reading the syllabus or specific assignments is of the utmost importance. This is because proactive students who take responsibility for their own learning succeed more often and on a greater scale than those who simply complain or expect others to magically read their minds. Do not wait for someone else to intervene on your behalf. You want to have all the information, and as a student it is your right to be informed and have your questions answered in a timely manner. Still, if you do not fully understand the course materials or what the instructor expects, it is your job as the student to ask for clarification.

Ultimately, your academic progress and success is your responsibility, and it is up to you to advocate for yourself. It is up to you to be timely with your concerns and communicate them to your instructor as soon as you realize you do not understand something on the syllabus or in class. More often than not, your instructor will appreciate your initiative and candor, and gladly assist you.

Instructor Expectations

It is not uncommon for instructors to consider the syllabus to be a contract with students; for others, it is more of an agreement. It should tell you—even if you have to read between the lines—what you need to do to excel in the class. That is why it is so important to read it, reread it, and continue to refer to it throughout the semester.

Threaded Discussions

Threaded discussions are common in online and face-to-face classes. A threaded discussion board or bulletin board system is a virtual space where students and instructors can post and respond to comments or "threads" on any topic they choose. Such discussions are often used to increase communication between and among students and instructors and provide additional clarity for key concepts or information covered in class. Your instructor may use threaded discussions to hold office hours, offer students assistance for homework, clarify any omissions or mistakes from lectures, and also answer posted student questions quickly. Threaded discussion boards also may be used as a central place for graded, academic discourse among online students, much like a discussion section in a face-to-face class.

How Threaded Discussion Works

While you may tend to think of discussions as verbal exchanges, a threaded discussion is a written exchange between classmates and/or instructors. These online, asynchronous, instructor-monitored exchanges are easily accessible to students via Internet or the school's learning management system. Threaded discussions may require several days to complete, or they may be nearly real-time, meaning threaded discussion postings can be almost as immediate as verbal exchanges are in classrooms. When responses are not posted in a near real-time fashion, threaded discussions still collectively build on each other even when comments are posted nonsequentially.

Whether responding in "real time" or at a later date, students should prepare to discuss the topics intelligently, make an effort to participate by directly addressing the questions posed by peers and instructors, mindfully build on the posts of others, and contribute to the discussion through reasoned responses that draw on relevant experiences. This ensures that discussions are more deliberate and insightful than your typical in-class, impromptu discussions.

Threaded discussions foster educational dialogue and academic discourse by saving all postings for later review. While the use of the technology alters the traditional nature of student and instructor interactions, the payoff for participants is often greater. One drawback is that asynchronous threaded discussions tend to take much longer to complete than face-to-face discussions. For example, it may take a full 24 hours for all students to initially respond to a question or prompt, and these responses may or may not be in chronological order as threaded discussion sequentially builds on itself.

For example, some students may enter a particular discussion late and still want to make a point on a topic after most students have already moved on to a new thread or topic. While having to recall a previous day's discussion might not work in a face-to-face setting, threaded discussion provides a written record as reference to all participants. Threaded discussions tend to require more planning from instructors and students, and participant conduct tends to be more deliberate and spread out because of scheduling differences. The length of a threaded discussion usually depends on the topic at hand, though most instructors allow up to a week for a discussion to run its course.

Participating in Threaded Discussions

Threaded discussions are easy to create and reply to, and are most often used to post questions and allow posted responses, or to post work and allow feedback and comments from fellow classmates and instructors. If you post something on a threaded discussion board, others may comment directly regarding the statements made. You see this kind of back and forth commentary underneath many YouTube videos, for example.

The threaded discussion process is simple. Usually, a comment or "thread" is made on the first line (for example, a comment about a sonnet by Shakespeare). Following the posting of the comment, a classmate or discussion board user reads the first line and then decides to comment directly to the statement (perhaps agreeing or disagreeing with the initial post's statements about Shakespeare's sonnet). Thereafter another classmate or discussion board user may decide to comment on the original statement or post a comment referencing the response.

Students may also decide to post a new "thread" or string of comments that may or may not be related to the initial post or thread. When posting to threaded discussions, it is a good idea to title your post so others have an idea of what your comment is about. Do not simply title your discussion post "Discussion." Think carefully about what you are titling things, and give your work a descriptive title that hints at the topic of your post.

Engaging in Discussions

As a responsible student, it is important to contribute to the course discussion. The smaller the class, the more you should engage in discussions. Overall, students usually find that instructors who consistently use threaded discussion boards as a communication tool in their classes are more available to respond to students and are better able to use valuable class time to cover new concepts and ideas. You are a critical component of discussions, and your thoughtful input is greatly appreciated.

A big advantage to a course that includes threaded discussion is that they virtually replicate the natural and dynamic interchange among students and instructors that occurs in many face-to-face classes. There is no reason why this kind of beneficial interaction between peers should be missing in an online environment. Such discussions tend to evolve organically and often mimic Socratic questioning when instructors monitor the tone and tenor of the threads. (Socratic questioning challenges students' thinking by asking conceptual clarification questions to get them to think more about what they are asking and thinking. The questions help students naturally prove the concepts behind their arguments by asking simple but probing questions that get them to go deeper.) Such discussions are valuable to students because they foster discourse that builds knowledge, encourages questioning, and keeps the learning focused on the needs and responses of the students.

Tips for Posting to Threaded Discussions

If you are new to threaded discussions, it may take a while to get used to the process. It is important to pay attention to the start and end dates of threaded discussions so you can schedule the rest of your weekly events around them. Keep in mind that your instructor may assess and grade participation in threaded discussions in order to motivate the class and spur on performance and participation. This is in part because of the written nature of threaded discussions. Assessment and instructional feedback on threaded discussions is the norm since students and instructors can easily review the (written) discussion in detail after the fact.

While evaluation criteria vary from instructor to instructor and from program to program, threaded discussion grades may be based on how well you demonstrate knowledge of the topic or subject, your ability to interact well and often, the creativity and thoughtfulness of responses, your demonstrated ability to include new ideas or material into threads, and the number and length of your posts.

Threaded discussions may take the place of a test or more formal written assignment as well, and often provide you with constructive feedback designed to help you better understand the topic and help you reflect and improve performance in future threaded discussions. Most students enjoy the dynamic interaction with others that threaded discussions allow and find that the resulting personal connections enhance their online educational experience. Students also appreciate the reassuring regular feedback from other students and/or instructors.

Beyond being merely a mechanism for positive feedback and interaction, threaded discussions also address multiple learning preferences. Students who are shy or those who are less apt to shout out answers may benefit greatly from the inclusion of threaded discussions since they de-emphasize quick-fire responses, giving students ample opportunity to reflect on the discussion and really think through their responses to it. Students who dislike face-to-face discussions in class, where one or two students dominate the debate, will appreciate threaded discussions. Students cannot be cut out of a conversation unless they choose not to participate.

Working With Course Materials

Course materials for an online class may be the same as a traditional face-to-face class, or the materials may be in a digital format only. It is now common to have course materials available exclusively online. This includes online documents (PDFs or Word documents), websites, articles, blogs (and vlogs, or video blogs), and video and audio recordings. Most of your course material and communication for online programs will be housed within the parameters of the online course management system such as Blackboard Inc. or Moodle among others. There are several reasons for this. By using the platform your school provides, you avoid most technology compatibility issues that may arise with other means of sharing ideas and work. You also benefit from not having to exchange a string of e-mails to communicate, which avoids the delay and crisscrossing that often occurs with multiple e-mails.

Working in Groups

Though it may sometimes feel like you are all alone in online classes, group work can help change that and is often a central component of online participation. Online, hybrid, and distance learning group work is not always the simplest of collaborations. Reasons abound for the complexities attributed to "virtual" group work, but rest assured, success and collaboration can and will happen as long as you know what to expect and do your part.

Group Dynamics

Despite the negative stories you may have heard, group work is manageable (and often fun, too). Group projects can be positive learning experiences for all involved and prepare you for group collaboration in a professional setting. Students often benefit more from doing a given activity as a group than they would by doing it alone. Keep in mind when you are collaborating for a debate or researching issues, there is often no one right answer. Everyone benefits from the ability to incorporate multiple perspectives (whether you are analyzing current events, making cultural or literary comparisons, or looking at a case study). In addition, students often benefit from the power of the group when there is a lot of research to evaluate in a short period of time. In these instances, group collaboration or a jigsaw puzzle approach to the project is needed, with each student taking responsibility for one part of the whole project.

It all starts with communication. When you communicate well and are able to articulate, you help your group members and help build a strong sense of collaboration and community with others. Groups that create shared understanding about goals and objectives, task requirements and interdependencies, roles and responsibilities, and member expertise end up with consistently high quality work and high grades. Implementing the five keys to successful group work outlined below (Shachaf & Hara, 2005) will help ensure you and your group members are successful in your collaboration.

The Five Keys to Effective Group Work

1. **Communication:** Strong communication means group members and the group leader (if one is appointed) provide continuous feedback, engage in regular and prompt communication, and clarify tasks.
2. **Understanding:** Group members are sensitive to the needs and schedules of all members, and appreciate their suggestions and opinions. Members care about each other's struggles related to the project, and

express a personal interest in them. Though it may sound superfluous to some, getting to know each other is central to effective collaboration. Group members should not share intimate details of their lives with one another, but sharing photos and things like your educational objectives, career goals, and any knowledge associated with the project is encouraged.

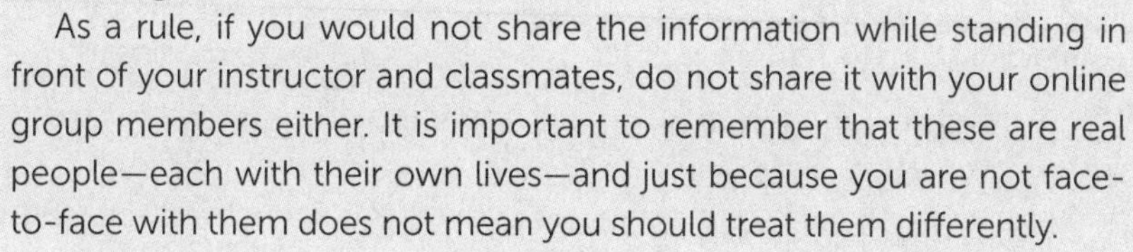

Sharing Personal Information

As a rule, if you would not share the information while standing in front of your instructor and classmates, do not share it with your online group members either. It is important to remember that these are real people—each with their own lives—and just because you are not face-to-face with them does not mean you should treat them differently.

3. **Role Clarity:** The responsibilities and jobs of all group members are clearly defined. It is not uncommon for one group member to take on a leadership role ("group leader") and help other group members who need additional guidance.
4. **Leadership Attitude:** Group members are proactive and assertive, but not overly "bossy." Group members are also caring, do their best to find common ground and relate to all other members of the group, and are consistent in their positive, proactive approach for the duration of the project and class.
5. **Listening:** Even when face-to-face communication is not possible, listening to one another is still a key characteristic of successful groups. The group dynamics may be different when you are meeting solely online, but listening by acknowledging communication (e-mails, chats, postings, etc.) and responding thoughtfully is important. All members of an online group work in isolation, which increases the need to pay attention to anxiety, concerns, and questions others may have within the group. Also, this is an essential skill needed in the work place—the ability to listen.

Once an online learning group project is assigned and group members are identified, it is essential to contact other members immediately to begin building a community within the group. Positive group dynamics is important to building a successful community relationship.

Establishing a reliable means of communicating with other group members is crucial if you want your group to be successful and for all group members to easily stay informed and on-task. It is usually best to agree on one central spot where members post their questions, comments, schedules, and feedback. In most cases, this will be located somewhere within your online course management system.

Setting up Protocol for Group Work

When working as part of a group, it is always a good idea to set parameters up front. Any confusion and frustration can be avoided when all group members know what is expected of them and the protocol for completing their share of the project. You may have to adjust your style or rearrange the manner in which you participate when completing group work. Repeating back what your group mates said can be a helpful way to ensure you have fully understood your role and the role others will have in the group project.

The availability of technologies such as teleconferencing, phones, texts, instant messages, and instant chat alongside traditional e-mail offer additional opportunities for communication. Cooperation can be enhanced with the creation of project websites, and wikis give groups a central digital repository for all collected project data and communication. Discussion boards or forums alongside work-sharing platforms (such as Google Docs™) are additional options for addressing group cooperation.

You might also wish to acquire outside means of communication as well. For example, using the web-based video-chat program, Skype®, for occasional "real-time" video chats when working on group collaboration helps make it easier for classmates to communicate with one another. With video conferencing or calling there is the added advantage of body language and facial expression in addition to mere written communication (which is sometimes misread). Logistics and concerns regarding coordination, responsibilities, and other questions regarding your collaborative project can be addressed during a Skype session. Plus, it is fun to see one another in "live time." It truly adds a new dimension to your online collaboration.

Online Collaboration: Strategies and Techniques

Beyond creating a strong foundation for open and regular communication, specific online collaboration strategies and techniques can help you and your group succeed. Simple transmission of information from point A to point B is not enough; the virtual environment presents significant challenges to effective group communication (Walvoord, Redden, Elliott, & Coovert, 2008). Being equipped with even the most advanced technologies is not adequate to make a virtual team effective, since the internal group dynamics and external support mechanisms must also be present for a group to succeed in the virtual world (Lurey & Raisinghani, 2001).

Obstacles to Effective Group Work

It is important for everyone to remember that the line between taking advantage of virtual technologies to enhance the quality of your learning and sharing opportunities and introducing additional (often unnecessary) complications into an online group project is one that can be easily crossed. The greatest stumbling block to effective online collaboration is not using selected technology properly (Mikkola, Niemelä, & Petterson, 2007).

Before you begin your collaboration in earnest, it is important to make sure all of your group members are comfortable using whichever technology platform the group selects. Everyone should have a say in which technology is used, and to what degree. Do not assume that just because group members are enrolled in an online class it means they are adept at computers and technology. The technical challenges that group members face, including compatibility of systems, security, and the selection of appropriate technologies, can make group work very challenging. Just because you like a certain tool does not mean everyone will. It is important to be thoughtful and careful when deciding on technology.

A basic understanding of group dynamics, teamwork, and successful online learning will help immensely. What is outlined for you here is just the tip of the iceberg. For more information, consult the book *Group Dynamics for Teams* by Daniel Levi, Ph.D. Reading it will open your eyes to a lot of hidden dynamics and underpinnings central to organizations and groups. Until then, the following tips should help you get there:

- **Clearly identify what everyone needs to do.** Be sure to come to consensus regarding tasks and distribution of workload. Along with establishing who will complete specific tasks, guidelines are needed for each task completion. This is fundamental to equal sharing of workload and successful project completion.
- **Clearly define and prominently post the roles of each of the group members in an established group forum.** This will avoid undue confusion over responsibilities and tasks for successful and on-time project completion.

- **Understand and be able to articulate how your work will be integrated and applied to the group project.** Doing so helps avoid a perception of busy work for some and overload of work for other group members. Everybody needs to do his or her part. No one group member should take on the heft of the project or be left out because of lack of ample communication.
- **Share your progress**. Early on, establish a means for sharing progress updates and develop a timeline for completion of tasks. This ensures everyone is working toward the common goal and avoids the temptation to wait until the last minute. Last-minute contribution by a group member is the main reason groups fail or submit lackluster collaborative projects.
- **Simplify, simplify, simplify.** Do your best to simplify complex project tasks into manageable steps. This relieves group stress and potential conflicts between group members, along with eliminating concerns some members may have regarding equal sharing of project workload.
- **Avoid overlap.** Be mindful not to overlap project tasks. This often leads to confusion regarding who is completing certain tasks and when.
- **There is no need to isolate group members or for you to feel isolated.** Do your best to engage regularly with others in discussions via e-mail or through other channels available to you. Clearly and constructively communicating your concerns as they arise helps everyone be aware of potential problems before they threaten to derail your project and success as a group and individually.

Awareness of common mistakes and the tools and strategies to avoid them increases your chances of success and cultivates positive feelings about collaborating with your peers. It also builds your teamwork skills and helps you gain valuable, real-world experience working with others, highly sought-after skills in today's global economy.

Keeping It Positive

A group of individuals, whether located in an office, classroom, or scattered around the globe, retains a basic need to develop social relationships.

Humans are social animals. In a very real way, the development of friendships, acquaintances, and interactions influences all aspects of their lives. This fact is at the core of the most frequent cause of virtual group failures. Although virtual collaborations are advantageous because they allow members to complete tasks while remaining geographically separated, the need for these teams to establish initial and ongoing positive relationships cannot be overlooked (Pawar & Sharifi, 1997). This is why virtual groups benefit from some form of "face-to-face" or live-time interactions.

Even a phone call to hear the other group members' voices has proven effective in establishing that initial bond. You have likely heard the expression, "There is no I in team," and the chance to see or hear one another is essential to the development of a sense of "team" for all group members engaging in online collaborations.

Searching Online and Accessing Resources

If you have ever used an online database or conducted an Internet search for an academic paper, you realize they can be both helpful and frustrating. While searching online may provide you with a wealth of information, not all of it is going to be high quality. Often, you find far too much information on a topic (though not necessarily the information you are looking for). There are a few reasons for this. Understanding the process and analyzing common stumbling blocks that occur when searching for academic research gives you a better chance to properly prepare and benefit from the search and avoid the common pitfalls of online searches.

Digital and Physical Resources

Sources of information abound in the current age. With so much at your fingertips, knowing where to start, sorting through it all, and finding what you want can often feel overwhelming. Before you begin your research, ask yourself some questions to help narrow your search parameters.

To begin, ask yourself what you want. Do you want facts? Opinions? News reports? Research studies? Analyses? Personal reflections? History? Which sources are likely to be most useful to you? Libraries? The Internet? Academic periodicals? Newspapers? Government records? How many sources of information are you looking for? Do you need to view both sides of the issue?

If, for example, you are searching for information on a current event, a reliable newspaper like *The New York Times* will be a useful source. Are you searching for statistics on some aspect of the U.S. population? Then, start with documents such as U.S. census reports. Do you want scholarly interpretations of literature? If so, academic periodicals and books are likely to have what you are looking for. Want to know about commercial products? Will those companies have websites with information? Are you searching for local history? Then a county library, government office, or local newspaper archive is likely to be the most useful.

One important distinction when doing research is the difference between traditional publications and Internet resources. Internet sources are published exclusively online in a variety of digital formats. These formats could be web pages, PDF documents, e-books, or other multimedia formats such as PowerPoint and video or audio recordings. The Internet may be the most convenient place to begin your research, but it is not always the best. One reason for this is because it can be difficult to determine the legitimacy and agenda of purely online sources. For example, if you did choose to research a company website for information on a product, the website likely will be biased to present the product and company in a favorable light. However, traditional publications include anything that has been published in print form and are widely available at libraries and bookstores. These materials include books, textbooks, newspapers, popular and scholarly journals, and magazines. While these sources could also have agendas and biases, they have the potential to be more reliable because of the standards in place for many of the types of publication.

Search Engines

A search engine is a device that sends out inquiries to sites on the web and catalogs any websites it encounters. Methods of inquiry differ from search engine to search engine, so the results reported by each one will also differ. Search engines maintain an incredibly large number of sites in their archives, so you must limit your search terms in order to avoid becoming overwhelmed by an unmanageable number of responses.

Since the Internet is made up of a vast number of computers networked throughout the world, new computers and websites are added many times a day. The Internet is dynamic and always growing, which makes navigating it quite challenging at times. This is where search engines and web directories come in. Search engines (like Google Inc. or Yahoo!) are large databases of information that store and retrieve relevant website results based on keywords. Web directories (like Open Directory Project) attempt to organize the best of the existing websites into categories and subcategories. Unfortunately, no search engine or web directory will have the same sites listed in the same order, and even the best search engines cannot possibly incorporate all Internet sites.

To complicate things even further, a website's rank within a search engine (how high up the site appears on the results list) has as much to do with politics and manipulation of search engine optimization tools as it does with sites containing high quality information. Search engine rankings are created based on factors such as the number of other sites that link to it, how many users end up selecting that link after searching, the length of time a search engine has listed the site, and the way the site is coded.

Lastly, search engines like Google and Yahoo! are funded by offering "sponsored links" to searchers. Sponsored links appear first on search results, that stand out (often bolded), and are paid for by advertisers. Instead of being interested in its relevance to your search, these search engines are more interested in paid advertising. The more you learn about the changing nature of the Internet and understand how it is organized, the better equipped you will be to filter information that is most relevant to your search.

Boolean Operators and How to Use Them

Most search engines allow you to combine terms with words otherwise known as Boolean operators. These are words such as "and," "or," and "not." Knowing how to use Boolean operators will greatly improve the chances of a successful search. Be sure to use a search engine that allows for an advanced search option if you want to incorporate Boolean operators to narrow your search results.

And

"And" is the most useful and most important term. It tells the search engine to find your first word "and" your second word or term. "And" can, however, cause problems, especially when you use it with phrases or two terms that are each broad in themselves or likely to appear together in other contexts. For example, if you would like information about the baseball team the Milwaukee Brewers and type in "Milwaukee *and* Brewers," you will get references to Milwaukee and to brewers or breweries. Since Milwaukee is one of the country's brewery capitals, many of the references will be about this since it is likely that "Milwaukee" and "brewers" will appear in many of the references relating to brewers and breweries. The team name should be thought of as a phrase, and therefore not split by "and."

Or

Use "or" when a key term may appear in two different ways. For example, if you are researching Type 1 diabetes, try "type 1 diabetes *or* Juvenile Diabetes." However, "or" is not always a helpful term because you may find too many combinations with "or." For example, if you want information on the 1984 Los Angeles Summer Olympics and you type in "Los Angeles Summer Olympics," thousands of references with the words "Los Angeles" and thousands of unrelated ones with the words "Summer Olympics" will flood your screen.

Not

"Not" tells the search engine to find a reference that contains one term but not the other. This is useful when a term refers to multiple concepts. For example, if you are working on a research paper on lions, you may encounter a host of websites that discuss the Detroit Lions football team instead. To omit the football team from your search results, you could search for "lions *not* Detroit."

Tips for Using Search Engines

In general, search engines help when looking for sources on well-defined topics. Typing in a general term such as "psychology" or "literature" will produce an unwieldy number of results, so knowing how best to narrow your topic and apply search terms is extremely helpful. Some search engines look only through page titles and the header (HTML [Hyper-

Text Markup Language] code that helps define the page), while others look through directories and portable documents as well (Google, for example, searches PDFs). Being specific about search terms and sticking to an appropriate search engine (for example, Google Scholar™ if you are looking for academically minded research) will help produce the type of information you want.

After trying several search engines, you will see that you get different results from different sites. Keep in mind that some information appears and then disappears from websites, and search engines do not always search the entire page. Employing a few basic search strategies and hints like the ones offered here will help you to secure useful and reliable online sources.

Mindfully Selecting Your Search Terms

It is important to gauge the number of results search engines offer and revise your search as needed. When facing too few responses, submit a more general search, and when faced with far too many, try adding more modifiers to garner specific results. Using inexact or vague, general search terms may produce a lot of results, but will cause problems almost immediately. When initial searches turn up myriad references, find a few relevant ones that may contain more exact terminology you can later plug into a new search. It is essential to rework and refine your search continuously, and make adjustments as your search evolves.

When struggling to make terms more precise, it can help to peruse a library's online catalog and try its subject word search or try searching the term in the online databases in the library. If you are looking to narrow a search based on specifics such as date, language, and type of file, most search engines offer an advanced search option that can help. It is also a good idea to learn how to use Boolean operators to aid you in your search.

A final note of caution regarding searches: even when a remarkable amount of information on a given topic is available online, it is essential to be mindful of the source and quality of the studies. There is often a very uneven level of quality research out there. Avoid sensationalized news stories and "fluff" stories. Online sites often want your money or want you to agree with their opinion (often disguised as fact), and see them as an expert, though they may lack credibility. It is your job to sift through the information and focus on information you deem to be credible, up-to-date, and reputable. Much like a trained detective, you are responsible for figuring out where to look for information, what clues to search for, and ultimately, what to accept as true and trustworthy. Avoid being overwhelmed by doing targeted searches, and do not simply accept whatever information you find as fact just because it is "in print."

Metasearch Engines

Metasearch engines search other search engines and tend to search smaller, lesser known search engines and specialized "niche" sites. Metasearches can be helpful when conducting broad searches regarding what kind of information is available. One drawback is that metasearch engines let you search only basic terms (no advanced search options or Boolean operators), and may not provide you with the most useful information since they can also pull results from pay-per-click advertisers.

Bibliographic Citations

When searching for information in library catalogues and online article databases (e.g., http://www.EBSCOHost.com), you will first see the bibliographic citation entries. A bibliographic citation provides relevant information about the author and publication as well as a short summary of the text. You should start with the citation and begin analyzing if the source meets your needs. Pay close attention to authors, title of the work, the summary, and the date of publication. You may also want to look at the keywords to determine other relevant categories. Evaluating this information first to see if it is valid for your research requires more work up-front, but is guaranteed to save you time overall.

Abstract Versus Full Text

Abstracts provide a useful summary of an article's (or other document's) contents. Often, abstracts are included with search results to help researchers identify relevant articles without having to read the full text. Be aware that databases may provide the abstract of a document and not provide the full text. Some abstracts can be very long and may look like the start of the full-text article; however, anything labeled "Abstract" will not be the full text of a document. If there is no link to the full-text document, then the full text is not available in that database.

Recognizing and Evaluating Scholarly Resources

Evaluating your sources is an essential step in any research activity. While the Internet can be an amazing resource, it does not contain all the information available at a library or through the library's database and online resources. While searching for information online is faster than physically searching through the library, it is not always wise to begin there unless you know how to leverage the Internet for your research objectives and are willing to take enough time and precautions to mindfully evaluate all the sources and information available to you.

Depending on the topic of your scholarly endeavor, there may be a large amount of information available, though much of it is probably unusable. Evaluating possible scholarly sources is an important skill, and it may help to think of it like detective work. Whether on the hunt for a suspect or a reliable scholarly source for your paper, it is up to you to decide where to look, what clues to search for, and what to accept as fact or fiction. You may have too many leads, or too few, and become easily overwhelmed with too much information, or frustrated by too little information. Just like a detective checking out a possible suspect, once you have found something, it is up to you to figure out if it is a valid or useful source. The way you go about doing that depends in large part on whether or not you are using print or Internet sources.

Print Versus Internet Sources

Today, many digital texts and sources are available online. The indexing of new websites and information (that is, finding and including new web pages and other media in a search engine's results list) is increasing exponentially. In 1994, for example, Google indexed approximately 20 million web pages. By the end of 2004, more than 8 billion pages were indexed (according to Google estimates). That number continues to grow at speeds almost impossible to comprehend. Yet Google and other search engines index only a fraction of what the Internet holds, and a lot of it may be outdated since search engines may only "crawl" sites (revisit sites for indexing purposes only) monthly. This means that information that was more recently updated will not show up in search engine results until the following month.

Some sources, such as journal and newspaper articles, are often available in both print and digital format. However, much of what is found on the Internet does not have a print equivalent, and may adhere to lower quality standards for publication online. This may be the result of self-publication by nonexperts, lack of peer review or oversight, or bias related to advertising. Understanding the difference between the types of resources available will help you evaluate what you find. Below is a comparison of print and Internet resources, highlighting the characteristics you can use to evaluate the quality of the information you find.

Print Sources

Publication information, such as date of publication, publisher, author, and editor, is always clearly listed in print publications, and clearly indicates who the author is, what organization(s) the authors are affiliated with, and when the work was published. Traditional print sources also go through an extensive publication process that includes editing and article review. The process has fact-checkers, multiple reviewers, and editors to ensure quality of publication. In most traditional publications, external sources of information and direct quotations are clearly marked and identified.

Furthermore, while bias certainly exists in traditional publications, printing is more expensive and difficult to accomplish. Most major publishers are out to make a profit and will not cater to special interest groups, or will almost always clearly indicate when they are doing so. In addition, qualifications of an author are almost always necessary for print sources, and only qualified authors are likely to have their manuscripts accepted for publication.

Below is a list of the most common research sources and a brief explanation of what information you can discover from each.

- **Books and Textbooks:** Books come in many topics. Because of the time it takes to publish a book, books usually contain more dated information than will be found in journals and newspapers.
- **Academic and Trade Journals:** Academic and trade journals are where to find the most up-to-date information and research in industry, business, and academia. Journal articles come in several forms, including literature reviews that examine current and past research, articles on theories and history, or articles on specific processes or research.
- **Newspapers:** Predominately covering the latest events and trends, newspapers contain very up-to-date information. Newspapers both report information that is factual in nature and also share opinions. Generally,

however, they will not take a "big picture" approach or contain information about larger trends.

- **Government Reports and Legal Documents:** An example of a government report is the U.S. Census data. Most government reports and legal documents can now be accessed online. In these reports, the government releases information intended for its own or public use. These types of documents can be an excellent source of information.
- **Press Releases and Advertising:** Companies, nonprofits, and special interest groups produce texts to help persuade readers to act in some way or inform the public about important news or recent releases.
- **Flyers, Pamphlets, and Leaflets:** Not all flyers, pamphlets, and leaflets are equally reliable. They should be evaluated carefully prior to use as they may be inaccurate or biased. In general, these can be useful for quick reference or very general information, but rarely qualify as quality references, and should not be relied on for serious research.

Internet Sources

Unfortunately, authorship and affiliations are often difficult to determine on the Internet. Some sites may have author and sponsorship listed, but many do not. This is because anyone with a computer and access to the Internet can publish a website or electronic document, and may do so anonymously or by using an unidentified pseudonym. In addition, many websites, online documents, articles, and blogs do not have editors, fact-checkers, or other types of reviewers. To complicate matters, the sources authors use or reference in text may not be clearly indicated.

Also pay attention to the stated (or unstated) purpose of the online text. It may be misleading. A website that appears to be factual actually may be mere opinion, or even worse, deceptive. Even if the author and purpose of a website can be determined, the qualifications of the author are not always given. Dates of publication and timeliness of information are questionable on the Internet. Keep in mind that all dates listed on websites can be altered, and sometimes a date may not be listed at all.

Of course with the advent of new technologies, many print resources also have an online component. Pay careful attention to whether the source you have found is an online-only source or if it has a print component as well.

Multimedia

Printed material is certainly not the only option for finding research. Also consider media sources such as radio and television broadcasts, interactive talks, and public meetings. The Internet has a multitude of multimedia resources including online broadcasts and news, images, audio files, and interactive websites.

Internet-Only Sources

- **Websites:** Most of the information on the Internet is distributed via websites. Websites vary widely in quality of information and validity of sources.
- **Weblogs/Blogs:** Weblogs or blogs are a type of interactive journal where writers post and readers respond. They vary widely in quality of information and validity of sources. For example, many prestigious journalists and public figures may have blogs, which may be more credible than blogs by nonprofessionals.
- **Message Boards, Discussion Lists, and Chat Rooms:** Discussion lists, chat rooms, and message boards exist for all kinds of disciplines both in- and outside of the university. However, plenty of boards exist that are rather unhelpful and poorly researched. Anyone with a computer and access to the Internet can contribute to message boards, discussion lists, and chat rooms. Many documents or forums on the web do not have editors, fact-checkers, or reliable review and publication guidelines in place.

Five Essential Strategies for Questioning and Evaluating Sources

After you have asked yourself some questions about sources you have found (and determined them to be worthy of your time to read and evaluate), it is your job to take a more critical look at the source information you are considering. The following tips and questions will help you with this very important step:

- **Skim the text first.** Look at the preface—what is the text trying to accomplish? Browse the table of contents and the index. This will give you an overview of the source. Determine the intended audience. Are you the intended audience? Is your topic covered in enough depth to be helpful? If you do not find your topic discussed, try searching for some synonyms in the index.

- **Consider the source.** How credible is the author? If the document is anonymous, what do you know about the organization and/or the website? Is this site or organization reputable? How do you know? Did you find any broad generalizations or oversimplification? Does the author use a good mix of primary and secondary sources for information?

- **Examine the evidence.** Is the content primarily fact, opinion, or propaganda? If you determine the source is offering facts, are the sources for those facts clearly indicated? If the source is opinion, does the author offer sound reasons for adopting that stance and support them? Is the coverage comprehensive? (As you learn more and more about your topic, you will notice that this gets easier as you become more of an "expert.") Are there vague or sweeping generalizations that are not supported with evidence? Are arguments very one-sided with no acknowledgement of other viewpoints?

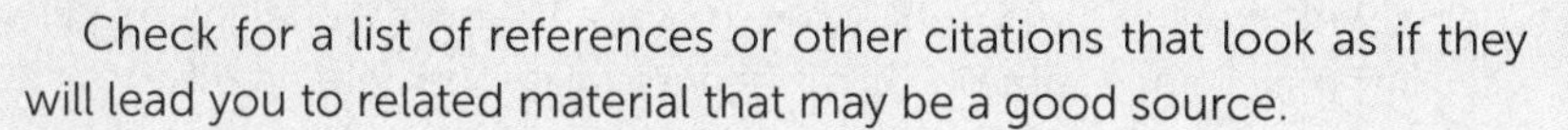

Works Consulted

Check for a list of references or other citations that look as if they will lead you to related material that may be a good source.

- **Look closely at language.** Examine the tone, style, level of information, and assumptions the author makes about the reader. Are they appropriate for your needs? Is the language and stance objective or subjective? Even or emotional?

- **Crosscheck.** How timely is the source? Is the source 20 years out of date? Some information becomes dated when new research is available, but other research and information can still hold up many decades later. Do some cross-checking. Can you find some of the same information given elsewhere?

Applying these five strategies before incorporating sources into your research paper or scholarly debate will help avoid many of the pitfalls students encounter when navigating the murky waters of online and print sources. You might want to print out the above checklist and position it near your computer as you continue to develop and evaluate your sources.

Summary

Today's students need to be savvy and sophisticated when it comes to working with school resources and scholarly sources for use in their academic careers. To avoid undue stress and conflicts, at the beginning of the semester it is always a good idea to compare syllabi for all your classes while you are entering due dates into your time-management system. Be sure to familiarize yourself with the syllabus and course materials early on.

In addition to the syllabus and course schedule, you will want to familiarize yourself with rubrics and other scoring tools for the course. Rubrics are tools that are sometimes used by instructors assessing your work and seeking an accurate grade or competency level related to a particular project, skill, or assignment in class.

Once you have begun your course, be prepared to participate in threaded discussions and group projects. Think of a threaded discussion as an ongoing conversation, only in print not oral form. Students are free to add to the discussion by posting responses or beginning a new post or "thread." Students who are shy or those who are less apt to shout out answers in the classroom may benefit greatly from the inclusion of threaded discussions. If you are new to threaded discussions, it may take a while to get used to the process, but you will.

And while online, hybrid, and distance learning group work is not always the simplest of collaborations, successful collaborations can and will happen so long as you know what to expect and do your part. For example, groups that create shared understanding about goals and objectives, task requirements and interdependencies, roles and responsibilities, and member expertise end up with consistently high quality work and high grades. Ultimately, your participation, academic progress, and success are your responsibility. It is up to you to advocate for yourself and promptly communicate any concerns or questions to your instructors and/or group mates; more often than not, your instructor and peers will appreciate your proactive initiative.

Anyone who has googled a topic of interest knows there is an ever-expanding plethora of information and resources available. It is even more essential that you pay attention to the type of sources you use and confirm you have reliable information to work with. When in doubt, review the strategies and checklist of questions about information you encounter both on- and offline. Remember the major points that determine the quality of a source, including whether information is produced by credible sources (experts or respected research institutions), whether there is convincing proof of the accuracy of the information, and whether there may be a bias that diminishes the source's objective reliability.

Remember, evaluating possible scholarly sources is an important skill, and finding the best sources for your needs is not unlike detective work. With the influx of digital sources, understanding the difference between resources available on the web and those found using more traditional print sources will help you find what you need and evaluate it. Be wary of anything without a listed author or identifiable source. And remember, while the Internet is a wild and wonderful thing, it is also growing at an exponential rate, and not all information there is created equally. Take the time to ask the right questions and understand where the information originates before using it for an academic assignment.

If you make it your goal to put forth your best effort in all your courses, your instructor and peers will likely do all they can to help you succeed. Make sure you participate consistently and communicate your questions and needs in a timely manner. Go beyond the minimum requirements, and be proud of the work you do each day. Your grade is a reflection of the quality and consistency of your work, your participation, and your overall attitude and aptitude in each course you are a part of. Do not underestimate the importance of your presence and contributions to class.

Section IV: Writing for the Online Environment

Beginning the Writing Process

In an online program, your writing is perhaps even more important than in a face-to-face program. As in any academic program, you will be required to write academic papers, but online programs also require you to write discussion postings. The word "discussion" may cause you to think that a discussion board, thread, or post has different criteria for the type of writing expected. In fact, the opposite is most often true. A discussion post, while different from a paper because of the robust back-and-forth engagement among students, should actually be considered academic writing. That is to say, casual style such as texting or instant messaging is not appropriate. This section covers good academic writing practice and process, which you can apply to both topical papers and your writing for online interaction.

Many students begin the writing process with much trepidation, whether they are writing an academic essay, discussion post, or creative writing piece. Engaging with ideas culled from others and learning how to treat those ideas with respect is one key to a great paper. But where to begin? Many students find that they can best bring ideas to the surface by writing freely with no restrictions about length, convention, or correctness. It is not a bad place to start. When you engage in this sort of pre-writing activity in order to "free" ideas from your mind, you allow space for original ideas and thoughts to take place.

> There will be time for revision later on—for now, just begin. Procrastination is the enemy of productivity, and starting writing is often the hardest part. Once you get past the vast white page, you are on your way, and it is up to you to decide the process that works best for you.

The Thesis Statement

Whether or not you engage in free-writing activities, you will want to begin all papers and essays with a clear sense of what your paper is about and why a reader would take the time to engage with your words. The key to a clear paper begins with a well-formed thesis statement. It should be a complete sentence that clearly conveys the point you plan to make in your paper. It should be broad enough to include all the ideas that are necessary as evidence but narrow enough to make a precise statement of your main point. If your thesis is too broad—for example "Shakespeare's portrayal of young love in *Romeo & Juliet* is very deep"—you will likely end up simply skimming the surface of the play and fail to provide a meaningful interpretation of the piece. Beyond the superficiality of the thesis, it falters on another count as well: It fails to make a real point.

A sound thesis statement for a paper on *Romeo & Juliet* may address one of several themes Shakespeare's play discusses and would be broad enough to make finding textual support easy, but narrow enough to provide a focused, clear point worth reading. A better thesis statement might be phrased as follows:

- Throughout *Romeo & Juliet,* Shakespeare reinforces the genuine nature of his young protagonists' love for each other through their words, deeds, and ultimate sacrifices.
- At its center, Shakespeare's *Romeo & Juliet* is a story about the undeniable power of love, and the ways in which love informs all aspects of our lives.

Most of the ideas and details you need to support any of these thesis statements will appear in the pre-writing or rough draft you have already completed. If you combine your thesis with a general statement about the work or topic, you should produce an acceptable introduction for a shorter paper.

Once you have formulated a solid thesis statement, you are ready to organize your ideas and material into a workable flow for composition. While there are many formats for organization, a basic but effective format contains three main parts: the beginning or introduction, the middle or body, and the end or conclusion. This three-step format works for nearly every kind of writing you will be asked to do.

The Basic Structure

The beginning or introduction of your paper has two primary functions: to pique your readers' interest and to convey the key point(s) you plan to make in your paper. The middle or body of your paper develops and supports the main point(s) with examples, reasons, details, and explanations that make the basic thesis statement more specific and understandable. The end or conclusion brings readers back to the main point by reiterating the core idea(s) your paper conveys and summarizing these points.

The Introduction

Your paper's introduction is your chance to make a strong first impression on your readers. A strong introduction is crucial to the effectiveness of your paper, and is often the most challenging to write. Your thesis statement is always part of the introduction, and should be easily identified by readers. If you are struggling with what to include besides your thesis statement, review your outline, which should provide a framework for your entire paper. If you have not written an outline, write one. Papers with outlines are generally much better organized and coherent than those written without one. Just because the introduction comes first sequentially does not necessarily mean you have to write it or complete it before the rest of the paper. Provided you have a clear thesis to work from, it is perfectly acceptable to work on the body of your paper before tackling the introduction. Many writers find that their best ideas come to them as they are writing or after they have given themselves a little wiggle room to work with before demanding the perfect introduction present itself. If you are stuck, consider tackling the body of your paper first. Whenever you choose to work on the introduction, it is important to work hard on your opening sentence so readers are engaged from the very beginning.

The Body

No matter what process you use to research and write your paper, organization and clarity are essential. Each topic sentence in the body of your paper should offer a critical observation relating to your main thesis. When writing the body paragraphs, it is important to state each critical generalization clearly and to support each with specific examples or references to make a convincing case. It is a good idea to relate a part of whatever it is you are analyzing to its whole. For example, in literary papers, it is wise to craft a thesis statement that makes its point by relating some aspect of the work to its theme.

Any good paper goes beyond offering a one-dimensional approach to an issue by making sure that the writing or research says something about the topic or story itself. No one taking the time to read an academic paper wants to read a mere summary or chronology of events. No one else thinks quite like you do, though—and that is your ticket to a good paper. You are going to be expected to illuminate and examine an issue; your unique observations and analysis are what make the paper worth reading.

Make sure that the details and examples you choose clearly relate to your thesis and help support and develop your argument. Examine your topic sentences and make sure they hold up—the topic sentence is usually the first sentence of the paragraph. Use the remainder of the paragraph to prove or support the critical generalization your topic sentence offers. Of course, you will have to decide which point to tackle first and which ones to use later as your thesis unfolds.

There are two main ways to arrange your topic sentences and body paragraphs: chronologically or logically. Chronological order is based on time and necessitates writing about events in the order in which they occur. Ordering your work chronologically may not work well for your particular topic, but most narratives and stories use a chronological approach. You may choose to use a chronological style when writing about literature or history, for example. When approached this way, your organization could simply follow the chronology of the work or discoveries you are writing about. Generally speaking, logical order is preferred in essays and academic papers because it offers a more analytical arrangement and helps keep your paper from reading like more of a summary than an analytical argument worthy of scholarly engagement.

Arranging your ideas in logical order means you are ordering points in a way that appeals to your readers' intelligence and good sense. It is common to begin with a less critical point and work up to the most important one. This is because your final point is the last one readers will be left with and the one they are most likely to remember, so it helps if it is the strongest. That said, you do not want to lose readers' interest in the beginning by giving them unimportant ancillary details and examples straight away.

The Conclusion

Your paper's conclusion is just as important as the introduction, if not more so. This is because you want to leave readers feeling satisfied knowing that they benefited in some way from what they read. A strong conclusion ensures readers are not left scratching their heads thinking "So what?" at the end of your paper.

While your conclusion should echo sentiments of your thesis, avoid simply restating your thesis statement at the end. A good conclusion offers a clear expression of the issue or theme that was offered as part of your introduction's thesis statement. It is a good idea to enforce the value of your paper and discussion by using the conclusion to show readers (as opposed to just telling them) how your research or analysis illuminates the meaning or theme of the work. Regardless of how worn-out you may feel by the time you compose your concluding paragraph(s), do not neglect your readers by leaving them with a weak conclusion. Work hard on that last sentence and make sure the end of your paper crystallizes the importance or meaning of your work, leaving readers with something to think about long after they have finished reading.

Writing With Academic Integrity

As you explore important questions and major debates in a variety of subjects and fields, you will be invited to join the scholarly conversation by composing your own papers and discussion posts. In order to contribute to the scholarly conversation, you need to understand how to use sources effectively and responsibly, and how best to avoid confusion and plagiarism.

Writing with academic integrity is an essential skill and absolutely critical to your success as a student. This is because most college writing assignments require you to respond in some way to scholarly sources. While some assignments require you to consult and incorporate only sources assigned in class, others will ask you to find your own sources relevant to a specific research topic or question. As you use sources with increasing sophistication, you will be able to confidently develop ideas of your own that are richer and more complex, and the entire endeavor of writing and researching will become much more rewarding. This can be tricky for novice academic writers, especially in the beginning when the rules of citing sources to avoid plagiarism are new. Luckily, resources abound to help writers avoid the pitfalls of plagiarism. Writing style guides (several discussed briefly later in this section) explain how to use and cite sources properly. Learning how to accurately cite your sources empowers you to write with confidence while giving credit to other scholars for their hard work and ideas, as well as assisting interested readers to learn more about your topic.

Most students have heard the word plagiarism before, but what exactly is it? In short, plagiarism is defined as the act of either intentionally or unintentionally submitting someone else's work as your own. If you turn in a paper that was written by someone else, or if you turn in a paper in which you have copied material from any source without citing that source, you are guilty of plagiarizing. Not knowing the rules is never a valid excuse. Student papers are an important part of academic discourse, and your written work will be held to the same standards as any other member of the academic community. When you fail to properly cite your sources, whether intentional or not, you commit plagiarism and risk your reputation and grade, and can put your entire academic career in jeopardy. This is because plagiarism is akin to stealing; however, instead of stealing tangible items, you are taking others' ideas and work and claiming them as your own.

You should familiarize yourself with the specific policy for plagiarism at your school or institution.

Put simply, the best way to make sure you do not plagiarize because of confusion or carelessness is to:

- Understand what you are doing when you write a paper.
- Follow a method that is systematic and careful as you do your research.

If you have a clear sense of what question you are trying to answer and what knowledge you are building upon, and if you keep careful, clear notes along the way, it is much easier to use sources effectively and responsibly and, most of all, to write a successful paper.

Remember that if you have questions about plagiarism at any point in your research or writing process, ask. It is always better to ask questions than to wait for an instructor to respond to work that you have turned in for a grade. Once you have turned in your final work, you will be held responsible for misuse of sources. The following tips will help ensure your papers are well-documented and written with academic integrity. Keep in mind this is not an exhaustive discussion but the most common pitfalls students make when writing academic papers.

Print Out and Keep Track of Your Sources

Keeping stack of books or journal articles on your desk and referring back to them is easy enough, but it is also essential to keep track of online and electronic sources. When you save a PDF of an article, for example, put it into a clearly labeled folder on your computer in an easy-to-find location. When you consult a website, add the address to an ongoing log, making sure you note the complete URL and the date you visited the website. You should also print the relevant pages since sites are frequently updated and revised.

Since electronic sources are not stable and web pages can be deleted without notice, beware of directing your readers to sources that might have disappeared. It is a good idea to keep track of when sites were last updated and check again just prior to submitting your essay. If an electronic source disappears, it is up to you to decide whether or not to keep the source in your paper. If you have printed the source and can turn it in with your paper, you are covered, but if you do not have a printout, be cautious. Remember the context in which the source or quote was given, and when in doubt, consult your instructor.

Know the Context

Ideas do not live in a vacuum. Be sure you understand the context of the ideas within a source, and the context of the source itself. For example, an anthology of American essays published by an organization with a religious or political bias may not offer a wide enough range of ideas or complexities for an academic paper.

Keep in mind that analyzing Internet sources is often trickier than print media. This is because you may be reading something published on a single web page that is part of a site. Though linked to the main site, if your Internet search takes you to that page directly, you may read the information on that page without fully understanding the context of the entire site. For example, a definition of "socialism" taken from a website with a particular political agenda may offer its interpretation of the definition that is not necessarily objective.

Think Ahead

Even for the most seasoned scholar, the research process often turns out to be more time-consuming than desired. Be sure to give yourself ample time to search for sources, take notes, and carefully consider which sources to use and how to use them. Honest mistakes can lead to charges of cheating or plagiarism. Be sure to be careful when note-taking and using ideas and language from online sources.

Do Not Cut and Paste

Avoid cutting and pasting words or whole passages from electronic sources directly into your paper, and do not simply retype sentences verbatim from sources straight into your essay. When tempted to do so, try the following technique instead. Open a new document on your computer for each source, and when you retype or cut and paste into that document, make sure to include the full citation details, including the whole URL and the date accessed if applicable. Remember to always use specific and logical names for your documents and files so you can easily retrieve them and avoid accidentally deleting files. Including the date as part of the file name can assist you in keeping track of the order you conducted your research in as well. When dealing with a lot of sources for a more involved paper, consider noting on each file how and where you think you will use the source information in your paper. Accurately naming your files helps you confidently enter into the dynamic process of engaging with and understanding your research sources as you build your argument.

Maintain Proper Boundaries

Writing with academic integrity requires you to vigilantly maintain clear boundaries. Always use quotation marks for directly quoted material, even for brief phrases and key words. For example, professor, poet, and activist M.K. Asante, Jr. discusses the rise of a new "post-hip-hop" generation in his best-selling book, *It's Bigger Than Hip Hop.*

As a writer and researcher, you should get in the habit of keeping your research notes separate from your actual paper; doing so ensures you do not omit language from a source and paste it into your paper without properly attributing it. If you work from separate notes as you draft your paper, it is a lot easier to keep track of where your ideas begin and end, and avoid blurring boundaries between your own words and ideas culled from outside sources. You should include detailed citation information in your notes as well.

Be sure to paraphrase material carefully in your notes and always acknowledge your sources explicitly when paraphrasing (regardless of whether or not the paraphrase is used in your notes or for the final product). While paraphrasing can be tough to do well, it is a critical art and skill to master. However, be sure to avoid excessive paraphrasing to ensure your paper is not simply one long string of paraphrased ideas. And unless you are a seasoned pro, it is always wise to first paste the actual quotation into your notes (not directly into the draft of your paper) and then paraphrase it (in your notes).

While this process takes a bit more work, translating the quote or information into your own words in your notes first ensures you have thought deeply about what is being said and why before including it in the final product. It also helps you to know whether or not your reason for using the source is sound.

Remember to use some form of notation when paraphrasing material within your notes, and always include the author's name within paraphrased material. This helps you guard against allowing words or novel ideas drawn from your sources to seamlessly blend in with your own writing. Always clearly indicate in your paper when the ideas are taken from an authored source.

Cite Now, Not Later

Avoid paraphrasing or quoting from a source without immediately creating a citation. Include thorough citations in all notes, drafts, revisions, and related assignments or response papers. Unless you are vigilant about adopting this "now, not later" attitude, it is far too easy to forget exactly where you found a good line, quote, or idea, and end up inadvertently plagiarizing.

Save Source Notes

As you write and revise your work, be sure to keep your sources up-to-date. Begin this source-note process early—preferably before beginning to write your first draft. Do not toss your notes after you turn in your work, either. Maintaining meticulous records and distinct boundaries between you and your sources drastically reduces the chances of accidental plagiarism. It is wise to keep all of your research notes and drafts at least until the end of the semester.

It is impossible to overstate the importance of maintaining academic integrity at every stage of the writing process. By now you know that plagiarism is a very serious offense. Plagiarism often results in failure of an assignment at the very least, possible failure for an entire course, and (in some cases) being permanently kicked out of the program or school. Do not hesitate to contact your instructor or a writing center tutor if you are unsure about how or when to cite a source.

Using Style Guides

Academic writing includes using specific paper formatting styles and following accepted rules for citing sources. The top three formatting style guides used in a variety of fields are MLA (Modern Language Association) style, APA (American Psychological Association) style, and the Chicago Manual Notes & Bibliography style (NB). Learning how to incorporate ideas and sources properly using a variety of styles is essential to your academic success.

Here is an overview of the three most used style guides. If you have questions about how to format your paper, ask your instructor, a writing tutor, or other writing and research experts in your field.

MLA Style

While in college, the MLA style tends to be the most widely used to write papers and cite sources within liberal arts and humanities. MLA style specifies guidelines for formatting and properly using the English language in writing papers. MLA style also serves an important function by providing you with a system for referencing your sources through parenthetical citation throughout your paper and on the final Works Cited pages.

Learning to properly use MLA immediately builds your credibility by demonstrating accountability to your sources. Most importantly, the use of the proper style protects you from accusations of plagiarism. While what follows is an overview, if you are asked to use MLA format, you should first consult the *MLA Handbook for Writers of Research Papers* (7th edition). Publishing scholars and graduate students should also consult the *MLA Style Manual and Guide to Scholarly Publishing* (3rd edition). The preparation of papers and manuscripts in MLA style is covered in chapter four of the MLA Handbook, and chapter four of the *MLA Style Manual*. Below are some basic guidelines for formatting a paper in MLA style.

General MLA Guidelines

- Double-space the text of your paper, and use Times New Roman 12-point font.
- Leave only one space after periods or other punctuation marks (unless otherwise directed by your instructor).
- Set the margins of your document to 1 inch on all sides.
- Indent the first line of paragraphs 1/2 inch from the left margin. Use the Tab key instead of pushing the Space Bar five times.
- Create a header that numbers all pages consecutively in the upper right-hand corner, 1/2 inch from the top and flush with the right margin. (*Note:* Your instructor may ask that you omit the number on your first page. Always follow your instructor's guidelines.)

- Use italics throughout your essay for the titles of longer works.
- If you have any endnotes, include them on a separate page before your Works Cited page. Title the section Notes (centered, unformatted).
- Type and print your paper on standard, white, 8.5 × 11-inch paper.

Formatting Your Paper in MLA Style

- Do not make a title page for your paper unless specifically requested.
- In the upper left-hand corner of the first page, list your name, your instructor's name, the course, and the date. Again, be sure to use double-spaced text.
- Double space again and center the title. Do not underline, italicize, or place your title in quotation marks; write the title in Title Case (standard capitalization), not in all capital letters.
- Use quotation marks and/or italics when referring to other works in your title, just as you would in your text: *Romeo & Juliet* as Love's Most Enduring Play; Human Folly in "A Good Man Is Hard to Find."
- Double space between the title and the first line of the text.
- Create a header in the upper right-hand corner of subsequent pages that includes your last name, followed by a space with a page number; number all pages consecutively with Arabic numerals (1, 2, 3, 4, etc.), 1/2 inch from the top and flush with the right margin.
- Consider using section headings to improve a lengthier paper's readability. These sections may include individual chapters or other named parts of a book or essay.

If using only one level of headings (no sub-sections fitted within sections), MLA recommends that sections mimic one another grammatically. For example, if your headings start off as short phrases, make sure all of your headings are short phrases. If you employ multiple levels of headings (some of your sections have sections within sections), consider including a key of your chosen level headings and their formatting for readers. Above all, just remember that formatting should be consistent and even throughout your paper.

APA Style

APA is most commonly used to cite sources within most social sciences. Below are examples for the general formatting of APA research papers, in-text citations, endnotes/footnotes, and reference pages. For more information, please consult the *Publication Manual of the American Psychological Association* (6th edition, second printing).

General APA Guidelines

Papers should be typed and double-spaced on standard-sized paper (8.5 x 11-inch) with 1-inch margins on all sides. APA recommends using 12-point Times New Roman font. Include a page header (also known as the "running head") at the top of every page. The running head is a shortened version of your paper's title and cannot exceed 50 characters including spacing and punctuation. To create a page header/running head, insert page numbers flush right. Then type the title of your paper in the header and flush left using all capital letters (i.e., TITLE OF YOUR PAPER).

Paper Sections

APA-style papers should include four major sections: Title Page, Abstract, Main Body, and References. The title page should contain the title of the paper, the author's name, and the institutional affiliation (your college or university). Include the page header (described above) flush left with the page number flush right at the top of the page. On title pages, your page header/running head should look like this:

Running head: TITLE OF YOUR PAPER

Pages after the title page should have a running head that looks like this:

TITLE OF YOUR PAPER

Type your title in upper and lowercase letters centered in the upper half of the first page. APA recommends that titles are less than 13 words in length and contain no abbreviations or words that serve little purpose. Your title may take up one or two lines. Beneath the title, type your name: first name, middle initial(s), and last name. Do not use titles (Dr.) or degrees (Ph.D.). Beneath your name, type the institutional affiliation, which should indicate the location where you conducted your research. All text should be double-spaced.

Abstract

Your abstract should be a single paragraph, double-spaced, and between 150 and 250 words.

Always begin a new page for the abstract. Your abstract page should already include the page header. On the first line of the abstract page, center the word "Abstract" (no bold, formatting, italics, underlining, or quotation marks). Beginning with the next line, write a very concise summary of key points of your research. Do not indent. Minimally, your abstract should contain your research topic, research questions, participants, methods, results, data analysis, and conclusions. You may also include implications of your research and future work connected with your findings. A list of keywords from your paper is also often included in an abstract. To do this, indent as you would if you were starting a new paragraph, type *Keywords:* (italicized), and then list your keywords. Listing your keywords makes your work more accessible to researchers when looking through databases.

Chicago Manual of Style

Chicago style is often used in the humanities and provides a system for referencing your sources through footnote or endnote citations in your paper and bibliography pages. It also offers writers an outlet for commenting on those cited sources. The Notes-Bibliography System (NB) system is most commonly used in the discipline of history and the arts. The proper use of the NB system can protect writers from accusations of plagiarism and helps build credibility by demonstrating accountability to source material. If you are asked to use the Chicago NB format, be sure to consult *The Chicago Manual of Style* (17th edition) and/or *A Manual for Writers of Research Papers, Theses, and Dissertations* (7th edition).

The Chicago Manual of Style (CMS) covers many topics from paper publication to grammar, usage, and documentation, and is often referred to as "the editors' bible." Technically there are two Chicago styles: the Notes-Bibliography System (NB), which is widely used by those in literature, history, and the arts, and the Author-Date System, which is preferred in the sciences. The Author-Date System contains almost identical content to the NB format, and differs only slightly in form. This section focuses solely on the NB System.

Notes-Bibliography System

Chicago's NB system requires writers to include a note (either endnote or footnote) every time a source is used. This includes all paraphrases, summaries, or direct quotes. Footnotes are included at the end of the page on which the source is referenced, and endnotes are compiled at the end of the paper or chapter. A superscript number corresponding to a note with the bibliographic information for that source should also be placed in the text following the end of the sentence or clause in which the source is referenced. Word processing programs may generate superscript numbers automatically when creating endnotes or footnotes.

The first note for each source should include all relevant information about the source: author's full name, source title, and facts of publication such as the year published, and the publication company and city. If the same source is cited again, the note only needs to include the last name of the author, a shortened form of the title (if more than four words), and page number(s). When consecutively citing the same source and page number(s) from a single source, the corresponding note should use the word "Ibid.," an abbreviated form of the Latin "*ibidem,*" which means "in the same place." If the same source is used but with a different page number, the corresponding note should use "Ibid." followed by a comma and the new page number(s). In the NB system, the footnote or endnote itself begins with the appropriate number followed by a period and then a space.

Bibliographies

In the Chicago NB system, the bibliography provides an alphabetical list of all sources used in a given work. This page, most often titled "Bibliography," is usually placed at the end of the work preceding the index. It should include all sources cited, and writers may also wish to include other relevant sources that were not cited but could provide further reading on the topic. Although bibliographic entries for various sources may be formatted differently, all included sources (books, articles, websites, etc.) are arranged alphabetically by author's last name. If no author or editor is listed, the title or keyword by which the reader would search for the source is used instead.

Contrary to the main paper, the author's name is inverted in the bibliography, which means the last name is first and separated from the first name by a comma. For example, Stephen King becomes King, Stephen. (If an author is not listed first, this applies to editors, compilers, translators, etc.) Titles of books and journals are italicized. Titles of articles, chapters, poems, and so forth, are placed in quotation marks. Remember, all entries in the bibliography must include the author (or editor, compiler, or translator), title, and facts of publication. The year of publication is listed after the publisher or journal. Please consult *The Chicago Manual of Style* for additional information.

Writing for Clarity

Seasoned writers continually ask themselves how they can make their writing clearer and more succinct. Just because you are writing a scholarly paper does not mean you should strive for an unnecessarily long paper filled with fancy words and convoluted sentences. The best writers say more with less. Shakespeare knew this, too, having famously penned the phrase so many writers and editors hold dear: "Brevity is the soul of wit." Many students make the mistake of relying too heavily on thesauri and the passive voice. While generally you do not want to write in the same style you speak, purposely using overly complicated structures to affect a formal "academic" or detached tone is not good practice either. It does not ensure that a paper achieves credibility; but it may ensure that the paper becomes unnecessarily dull and difficult to read.

While a lively paper certainly varies sentence structure from time to time, your writing should not be so complicated that it buries the thesis and main points. In general, the clearer and more direct your writing, the better your paper. Even when tackling the most complex issues, papers could almost always be improved by making the writing more succinct, direct, and active. The following tips are suggested with clarity and directness in mind:

- Use active voice rather than passive voice whenever possible.
- Do not begin sentences with unwieldy and filler phrases like "it is imperative."
- Get right to the point and avoid long drawn-out prefacing.
- Make sure the subject of the sentence is easily identifiable.
- Do not rely on long lists of items all prefaced with the same phrase.
- Eliminate clichés and other overly used expressions from your writing.
- Avoid opening sentences beginning with "it is" or "there are." These expressions rarely add anything to the meaning of the sentence.
- Outline the paper before and after writing it.

This last one might sound a little strange—outlining your paper before and after you write it? The reason for this is simple. Creating an outline based on the draft after the paper is written enables you to step back from your writing and really examine what is there. Practicing this step makes you a more objective, and thus better, critic. It is a straightforward process. Simply state the thesis, and then put this idea at the top of the outline. Then, go through the paper, pulling out the main ideas and supporting evidence from each paragraph to compose the body of the outline. Doing so helps you get a general idea of the paper's movement, thus elucidating the main points of each idea. This "backward" outline helps you decide what to keep, what to cut, and which parts need to be rearranged, moved, or more thoroughly incorporated into the paper and its thesis.

The following questions and guidelines are designed to help you evaluate the first draft of a paper. If you are not required to have your paper peer evaluated, consider visiting your institution's writing center, or ask a tutor or trusted friend to read and evaluate your paper, keeping the following questions in mind:

- Does the paper have a clear purpose? Is that purpose reflected in a strong thesis statement?
- What is the main point(s) of the paper? Does the whole paper clearly relate to the main point(s)? Is the main point compelling or too generic and predictable?
- Are the ideas expressed clearly and consistently throughout? Make note of words or passages you find confusing. Notice if there are sentences or paragraphs you keep rereading to make sense of them.
- Does the paper have enough substance? Do some ideas need more details or support? Make note of places that lack depth or sufficient support, examples, or detail. Pay attention to any "leaps" in association or cause and effect and to places in the paper where your attention starts to drift.
- Does the paper have a good flow? Are there clear transitions between points? Are ideas and paragraphs well organized throughout? Does the order of body paragraphs need to be rearranged? Are there paragraphs or ideas that do not seem to belong with the rest of the paper? Do the opening and closing need revision? What impression are you left with at the end of the paper? Does the last line effectively conclude the paper?
- Is the tone and format consistent throughout? Are you distracted by improper grammar, sentence structure, or typographical errors? Take note of any overuse of words or phrases. Is there proper subject-verb agreement in all sentences? Do you notice discrepancies in tense? Note

areas where words or phrases are clichéd, unnecessary, or used improperly. Are all quotes accurate and contained within quotation marks? Is the sentence structure logical? Is there ample sentence variety?

Checking Grammar

Your written assignments are generally graded on four key areas: how well you have handled the topic and followed the assignment, the quality of your ideas, your paper's organization and flow, and the quality of your writing style and grammar. This means that grammar is only one of a number of factors determining your grade. Still, allow too many errors in grammar, punctuation, and style and you risk a significantly lower grade. The reason for this is simple: How you use grammar reflects your writing skills and will give the reader an indication of the content in the paper.

When used skillfully, punctuation provides you with considerable control over meaning and tone. The most common grammatical mistakes involve punctuation. Commas and apostrophes confuse a lot of people. There are either too many commas or not enough, and sometimes they are incorrectly used or omitted. Apostrophes have fewer uses than commas, but people still misuse them. To confuse matters, there are many words in the English language that sound the same but have different meanings. You should take great care when reviewing your essay to ensure the word used is the proper word for the sentence.

Pronouns can also challenge writers. The pronoun should match the noun it is identifying, whether it is singular or plural. However, the most common pronoun mistakes fall within the sentence structure. There are pronouns that are used in the subject portion of the sentence and ones that are in the predicate portion of the sentence. A quick review of pronoun usage will also help you when editing your essay. Of course, there are other grammatical errors writers make that can give the reader a bad impression of the writer and his or her ability. Typos, misspellings, and sentence fragments are among the top grammatical mistakes made in academic essay writing.

No one's grammar is perfect, but it is important and expected that you put forth your absolute best effort in academic writing. If you are not careful and have not taken the time to consider grammar, spelling, and mechanical issues, the paper will reflect poorly on you as a writer. If you need to brush up on grammar, most schools offer resources for students looking to improve their skills. It is never too late to learn. Improving your grammar ensures you write with confidence and clarity, and this skill will pay off throughout your career.

Always use the grammar checker and spell checker prior to submitting a paper.

Summary

In an online program, your writing is perhaps even more important than in a face-to-face program since you will be required to write discussion postings rather than engage in a verbal discussion. Since your written words speak for you, it is essential to first understand and then convey a clear sense of your topic, and why a reader would take the time to engage with your words. Remember, the key to a clear paper begins with a well-formed thesis statement. A thesis statement should be a complete sentence that clearly conveys the point you plan to make in your paper.

Remember that most essays contain three main parts: the beginning or introduction, the middle or body, and the end or conclusion. The introduction of your paper has two primary functions: to pique your readers' interest and to convey the key point(s) you plan to make in your paper. The body of your paper develops and supports the main point(s) with examples, reasons, details, and explanations that make the basic thesis statement more specific and understandable. The conclusion brings readers back to the main point by reiterating the core idea(s) your paper conveys and summarizing these points. Using this three-step format works for nearly every kind of writing you will be asked to do.

Once you have a solid thesis statement, it is time to organize your ideas and material into a workable flow for composition. Make sure that the details and examples you choose clearly relate to your thesis and help support and develop your argument. Examine your topic sentences and make sure they hold up—the topic sentence is usually the first sentence of the paragraph. Use the remainder of the paragraph to prove or support the critical generalization your topic sentence offers.

Your written assignments are generally graded on four key areas: how well you have handled the topic and followed the assignment, the quality of your ideas, your paper's organization and flow, and the quality of your writing style and grammar. Typos, misspellings, and sentence fragments are among the top grammatical mistakes made in academic essay writing.

Take the time to check grammar, spelling, and mechanical issues: The paper will show it. In general, the clearer and more direct your writing, the better your paper will be.

If you are not required to have your paper peer evaluated, make an appointment with the writing center or ask a tutor or trusted friend to go over it with you one last time before submitting it for a grade.

It is also important to familiarize yourself with the most commonly used formatting guides: MLA (Modern Language Association) style, APA (American Psychological Association) style, and the Chicago Manual Notes & Bibliography style (NB). Your institution's writing center can help you to comply with their required style.

Perhaps most importantly, writing with academic integrity is critical to your success as a student. It is essential to properly use sources effectively and responsibly to avoid confusion and plagiarism.

Section V: Finishing the Course

Practical Applications: Professional and Personal

Congratulations on finishing your online course! You took a big step forward by boldly venturing into the world of online learning and successfully completing your course. The first online course is often the most challenging because everything is new.

You had to learn new technologies, adapt to a virtual environment, and spend time developing new habits and systems. It was not easy, but you did it.

Even in light of your success, if the experience still has you feeling nervous about continuing with online coursework, do not give up without giving yourself time for careful reflection. Online education programs are becoming the new norm with more than 3,300 of the 4,500 colleges and universities in the United States offering online courses, according to a 2009 survey by Babson Survey Research Group. However, succeeding in an online course takes patience and practice. Even the most successful students experience stretches during their academic career where they question whether or not they have the gusto to follow through. Sharing these feelings with friends and trusted family members can help you through the rough patches. Do not be afraid to talk about things with an academic advisor, instructor, or mentor. When you approach future courses without hidden fears, you are at a distinct advantage over students who enroll in courses without much forethought. Knowing what intimidates you and why, combined with realistic expectations of yourself and your time, will serve you well regardless of whether or not your future includes online learning.

Take some time to reflect on how you have advanced and take stock of what you have learned. School is a laboratory for life, and working in a group (whether in person or virtually) prepares you well for future collaborations. You have no doubt learned some new skills and managed to overcome common challenges facing online learners. It will be useful to transfer skills and concepts you have learned in your online course into practical applications for your professional and personal life and build on the personal connections you may have fostered with fellow classmates. Connecting with your classmates can help keep you motivated and buoy your spirits throughout your program. If you have been part of a virtual group, this experience may mimic the kind of work you are likely to face in the future. It is possible that many of you are already working with people virtually on group projects, whether it involves meetings via Skype, telecommuting, office conference calls, or e-mail correspondence.

Online group projects are an excellent chance to further develop the skills and confidence you already have to work within a group successfully. These include social skills and getting to know your teammates, learning to seek common ground, practicing communicating well via e-mail and online posts, and developing and refining a shared vision for your work. Hopefully you have also learned how to make virtual work feel more personal by taking a little time to share interests and tidbits about yourself with the rest of the group.

While taking online courses is not necessarily in every student's best interest, even the most reluctant online students feel more confident and adept at navigating virtual communication and the dynamic online world after ample time and practice. Keep in mind it is important to stay abreast of changes if you want to do well and succeed in future courses. This is true whether the course you have completed was just one of many online courses you have taken, or part of your first foray into the world of online education.

Getting Ready for the Next Course

Now that you are familiar with many of the tools used in online education, you are poised at a new juncture. Take a moment and imagine that your next online course starts next week. Do you know what to do before the first day of class? Anticipating what is to come and preparing in advance will not only keep you organized, it will allay many common fears and lessen the anxiety that comes from dealing with things at the last minute. Whenever possible, find out which courses and instructors you will be working with next in your program. By being proactive and thinking ahead, you will set yourself up for success.

It is important to remember that each course within a program is different, and that success in one online course does not automatically translate into success in other courses. If you fail to plan out your course of study well in advance, you can inadvertently put yourself in situations where the odds of being successful are not in your favor. The key to your success is in your preparation and planning.

Again, reflect on your experiences during your first course. What habits and methods did you find worked best for you? Think about how you can improve on them and use them in your next course.

Here are some important reminders to get you thinking. Contact your instructor after you enroll in your next course. Ask for a copy of the syllabus well in advance of the first day of class if not already provided. The syllabus is, by far, the most important piece of information you have. Syllabi should have information on your instructor's attendance and grading policies, any required materials and readings, your major assignments and subsequent due dates, as well as specific course objectives, teacher expectations, and desired learning outcomes.

Do not be shy about contacting your instructors ahead of time if you have questions after reviewing available course information. Most instructors will let you know how best to contact them. Many instructors send a confirmation or welcome e-mail once student rosters have been finalized. Your online instructors will provide you either with links to their websites, IM (instant messaging) addresses, Skype IDs, wiki and blog addresses, or office phone numbers. Make sure you know which way(s) your instructors prefer to be contacted, and always keep contact information close at hand.

Be sure you are familiar with the course management system. It may have been updated since your last online course. While all course management systems have similarities, they contain significant differences as well. Be sure to log in and understand where everything is located before the course begins. If you cannot login before the first day, be sure to dedicate some extra time to exploring the system that first week. Do not be afraid to click away; you will not hurt your computer or your school's course management system just by clicking on something.

If you run into issues, do a browser check. While certain course management systems are compatible with Safari, Firefox, or other browsers, most systems are designed to pair best with Internet Explorer. Experiment with logging in to your course and double-check that you can access all areas of the course management system that you will need for your online course. It would also be a good idea to do a "plug-in check" to ensure you have downloaded all updates and programs you will need in order to run required media for your program. Do you have the most recent versions of Adobe Acrobat, Flash®, Shockwave, QuickTime®, and Windows Media Player®? If not, this might be a good place to start.

Do not wait to order books and supplies. Whenever possible, buy or borrow the required books and course materials and look them over prior to the first day of class. Give yourself time to peruse the readings and skim the texts to get a better sense of the content and material your instructor hopes to cover throughout the course. This will help you know what is coming, and assist you in scheduling enough time to complete readings and work on time. Do not just squeeze in study time after everything else is off your to-do list. Think about all the demands on your time and determine when you are most alert and able to offer your studies your undivided attention.

While the idea of meeting deadlines can be intimidating, it is wise to set deadlines and goals for yourself to help you stay on-task and motivated. You do yourself a big disservice by studying and working in an unfocused, random manner. It helps to review personal deadlines and your course's non-negotiable due dates on a regular basis. It is also important to stay organized by setting up a system for work and files ahead of time. By anticipating your needs in advance and blocking out chunks of time, you help your future-self complete assignments on time.

Get into the habit of outlining a study plan and sticking to it. Remember that just studying the course material is often not enough—creating optimal study conditions are equally important. Will you be taking timed quizzes and tests? The best way to practice for an exam is to replicate the test conditions as closely as possible. Make sure you have a space that works for you—and only you.

If you struggle with getting started, break down larger assignments into separate and more reasonable tasks. Take a close look at any intimidating projects, assignments, or longer readings and think about how you can make the work more manageable. Before each study session, list specific outcomes you plan to achieve that day. Once you have finished a daunting task, reward yourself. Do a little something nice—just for you—after you have finished. Whether it is an afternoon with friends once you have written your paper, or a 15-minute walk in the sunshine after posting your outline, these little treats can go a long way when it comes to motivation and fostering a positive attitude and approach to your studies.

It can be tough to stay motivated in an online course that deals with a subject that is not inherently interesting to you, or if you feel disconnected from your instructor and peers. If this is the case, it is best to make any concrete concerns known as soon as possible. If you experience difficulties, have extenuating circumstances, or require special accommodations and have special needs you would like addressed, it is your responsibility as the student to notify your instructors as soon as possible (preferably prior to or at the beginning of the term).

While some of what you have heard about online programs may be correct, you may be surprised to find out that your online courses are very different from what you expected. It is important to know what works best for you as an online learner, and set realistic and attainable expectations for yourself and your courses. For example, it may be difficult to stay focused on your studies if you are working full-time and taking care of others on a regular basis. Figure out how to manage your time before you start your course. Large chunks of time to study and log on to class will not magically appear. Try to regularly set aside smaller chunks of time in which to study, read and post comments, and work on assignments. Do not feel you have to finish in one sitting.

If, like some online students, you feel disconnected or isolated, make a concerted effort to reach out to others in the course by posting something in a discussion forum or asking for a virtual study buddy. Look for points of interest for each course. Even if the subject bores you, try to make connections between the material you are covering and the work you are required to do, and your long-term goals or interests. Remind yourself of the rewards you will receive by achieving your goals.

As you continue working on current or future courses, review the tips, reminders, and guidelines outlined for you in the *Essential Guide to Online Learning*. Make sure you have the right technology and a designated study space. Set yourself up for success by doing research on courses, instructors, financial aid, and time obligations well in advance. Organize your course materials at the beginning of the course, and figure out ways to keep yourself motivated for the duration of the course. Before the course begins, make it clear to family and friends why you are taking the course, and how they can help and support you. Once you begin your courses, make it a priority to interact with other students online in a respectful and reliable manner, and cooperate with instructors and peers while participating in group work, discussion boards, and other online collaborations.

Reflecting on all you have done—and how—will better prepare you for the next course in your program. As with all endeavors, success comes only when you combine know-how with action time and time again. Putting all you have learned to work for you by being proactive in your studies is an important key to your success. With advanced planning and preparation, you will be poised to handle whatever comes your way with ease and grace.

References

Babauta, L. (2009). *The power of less: The 6 essential productivity principles that will change your life.* London, United Kingdom: Hay House UK.

Carnevale, D. (2002, July 19). Stronger students benefit more from online course, Texas study finds. *The Chronicle of Higher Education*, p. A30.

Fleming, N. D., & Mills, C. (1992). Not another inventory, rather a catalyst for reflection. *To Improve the Academy, 11*, 137–155.

Ko, S., & Rossen, S. (2010). *Teaching online: A practical guide* (3rd ed). New York, NY: Routledge.

Lurey, J. S., & Raisinghani, M. S. (2001). An empirical study of best practices in virtual teams. *Information and Management, 38*(8), 523–544.

Malhotra, A., & Majchrzak, A. (2004). Enabling knowledge creation in far-flung teams: Best practices for IT support and knowledge sharing. *Journal of Knowledge Management, 8*(4), 75–88.

McVay Lynch, M. (2002). *The online educator: A guide to creating the virtual classroom.* New York, NY: RoutledgeFalmer.

Mikkola, T., Niemelä, K., & Petterson, J. (2007). *The questioning mind: Faith and values of the new generation.* Tampere, Finland: Church Research Institute.

Palloff, R. M., & Pratt, K. (2001, August). *Lessons from the cyberspace classroom.* Paper presented at the 17th Annual Conference on Distance Teaching and Learning, Madison, WI. Retrieved from http://www.uwex.edu/disted/conference/Resource_library/proceedings/01_20.pdf

Pawar, K. S., & Sharifi, S. (1997). Physical or virtual team collocation: Does it matter? *International Journal of Production Economics, 52*(3), 283–290.

Shachaf, P., & Hara, N. (2005). Team effectiveness in virtual environments: An ecological approach. In S. Pixy Ferris & S. Godar (Eds.), *Teaching and learning with virtual teams* (pp. 83–108). Hershey, PA: Information Science Publishing.

Walden University. (2012). *Student readiness orientation: Time expectations for online learning.* Available from http://www.waldenu.edu/

Walvoord, A. A. G., Redden, E. R., Elliott, L. R., & Coovert, M. D. (2008). Empowering followers in virtual teams: Guiding principles from theory and practice. *Computers in Human Behavior, 24*(5), 1884–1906.

Bibliography/Resources

Bowman, L. (2010). *Online learning: A user-friendly approach for high school and college students.* Lanham, MD: Rowman & Littlefield Education.

Dunlap, J. C. (2005). Problem-based learning and self efficacy: How a capstone course prepares students for a profession. *Educational Technology Research and Development, 53*(1), 65–83.

How to master online learning. (2010). Lawrenceville, NJ: Peterson's.

Swan, K. (2009).Threaded discussion. In P. L. Rogers, G. A. Berg, J. V. Boettcher, C. Howard, L. Justice, & K. D. Schenk (Eds.), *Encyclopedia of distance learning* (2nd ed., Vol. 4., pp. 2110–2118). Hershey, PA: Information Science Reference.

Tobias, S. (1992). *Revitalizing undergraduate science: Why some things work and most don't.* Tucson, AZ: Research Corporation.

Watkins, R., & Corry, M. (2011). *E-learning companion: A student's guide to online success* (3rd ed.). Boston, MA: Wadsworth, Cengage Learning.

Glossary

Academic Integrity: Moral and ethical principles, including avoidance of plagiarism, applied to academic endeavors.

Active Listening: Being mindful and giving full attention to the present moment and what the speaker is saying. Good active listeners prepare for the discussion or exchange in advance.

Active Reading: Reading with intent. The intent is the purpose and framework for the reading. Focusing on the larger purpose and intent to gain a better understanding of the content.

Active Versus Passive Voice: In passive voice, the subject of the sentence does not "do" the action. If the reader knows the agent of the action, as in active voice, writing is clearer and stronger.

Address Bar: The field at the top of a web browser where you enter the URL for the website you want to view. For example, if you want to visit Yahoo!'s main site, you would type http://www.yahoo.com in the address bar.

American Psychological Association (APA) Style: Scholars in social and behavioral sciences use APA style. Fields of study include business, education, nursing, and social work.

Asynchronous Course or Program: A class or program where students are not required to log into class at the same time. A distance learning or correspondence course is another type of asynchronous course because assignments are mailed to the instructor, assessed, and then returned to the student via postal mail.

Attachment: A file sent with an e-mail. Almost any file type can be sent as an attachment (Word documents, image files, spreadsheets, etc.), and it is possible to attach multiple files to the same e-mail.

Bibliography: A list of the works a writer consults as background in a research project. It may include descriptive notes and recommend further reading.

Blog: A "web log," or website, usually containing journal-type entries by a "blogger," or writer. Some blogs have multiple bloggers (writers) and readers of the blog are usually able to leave comments on individual blog posts. Commenters may have to give a name, set up an account, type a brief phrase, or provide some contact information so the blogger knows you are not a spammer.

Boolean Operator: Most search engines allow you to combine terms with words such as "and," "or," or "not." Knowing how to use Boolean operators will greatly improve the chances of a successful search.

Browser: A software application that allows you to access Internet content. Internet Explorer, Firefox, and Safari are all examples of browsers.

Cache: (pronounced "cash") A location on your computer where files are stored temporarily for quick access. When you visit a web page, the page is stored in the cache directory on your hard drive. If you want to return to the page later, the browser can retrieve it from the cache rather than from the page's server.

Chicago Style: Chicago style is often used in the humanities and provides a system for referencing your sources through footnote or endnote citations in your paper and bibliography pages. It also offers writers an outlet for commenting on those cited sources. Technically there are two Chicago styles: the Notes-Bibliography System (NB), which is widely used by those in literature, history, and the arts, and the Author-Date System, which is preferred in the sciences. If you are asked to use the Chicago NB format, be sure to consult *The Chicago Manual of Style,* 17th edition and/or *A Manual for Writers of Research Papers, Theses, and Dissertations,* 7th edition. The Author-Date System contains almost identical content to the NB format, and differs only slightly in form. The Chicago Manual of Style (CMS) covers many topics from paper publication to grammar, usage, and documentation, and is often referred to as "the editors' bible."

Citation: A reference to the source of the quotation or content designed to acknowledge the author(s) of the original work. Every writing style (APA, MLA, etc.) has its own system for citing work within a text or paper.

Cookie: A special text file that a website puts on your hard drive so that it can remember something about you at a later time. A cookie records your preferences when using a particular site. For your online courses, cookies are used to manage your user ID and password information whenever you log in to the site.

Desktop: The main screen of the Windows and Mac operating systems. After you have logged in to your computer, the desktop is the first screen you see. The desktop displays icons, which are small picture representations of programs or files.

Digital Media: All types of digital content including text, video, audio, and graphics transmitted electronically on a computer using software, Internet, or computer networks.

Firewall: A set of related programs designed to prevent unauthorized access to a computer or computer network through an Internet connection.

Frame: An independently controllable section of a web page. While a web page may look like a single page, it may be several pages combined, each in its own "frame." You may be able to "scroll" through text in one frame without affecting any other frames. Your online classroom has two frames: one with the navigation tree and one where the course content appears.

Hard Drive: (also referred to as a "hard disk drive") It is usually the main storage device of your computer. It holds the operating system and any programs that have been installed on the computer. You can save your work to the hard drive (usually designated as the "C" drive).

Hardware: The physical components of computers and related devices. Your monitor, modem, and keyboard, as well as the computer itself, are all examples of hardware.

Hybrid Course or Program: Hybrid classes and programs use a combination of technologies and delivery methods to provide students with optimal learning opportunities. Many hybrid programs consist of some actual face-to-face instruction combined with online components such as e-classrooms, telecourses, virtual chatrooms, and other e-tools.

Hyperlink: A connection between one document or web page and another or between sections within a document or website. Clicking on a "link" takes you to the new location.

Instant Message (IM): Real-time text messages.

Internet: A worldwide system of computer networks in which any one computer can, if it has permission, get information from any other computer (and sometimes talk directly to users at other computers). The Internet is a public, cooperative, and self-sustaining facility available to millions of people worldwide. While commonly confused, the Internet is not the same as the World Wide Web. The Web is part of the Internet.

Internet Service Provider (ISP): A business that provides access to the Internet. An ISP is a service you normally pay for, similar to service with a phone company. An ISP may also give you an e-mail account. Examples of ISPs include Verizon, Charter Communications Holding Company, LLC, and BellSouth Corporation.

Learning Styles: Your learning style is the way you prefer to learn. Learning styles are most often broken down into four categories: Visual, Aural, Read/Write, and Kinesthetic (VARK). Multimodal (MM) is considered a fifth learning preference, and is a combination of the four VARK styles.

Log in: The process of entering identifying information into a computer program to gain access. When you log in to your course, your computer is connecting to the computer where your institution's online data is stored. (The one-word term "login" is often used to mean a person's user ID.)

Media Player: Software that delivers media content, including video and audio, through streaming media channels or through downloads directly to your computer or mobile media device, such as a compatible cell phone. Video and audio media are used extensively in online programs. Most institutions provide some type of media player for students to use to access this content.

Metasearch Engine: A search engine that searches on multiple search engines and aggregates the results into one list.

Modem: A device that allows you to connect to the Internet through an analog phone line or a cable connection, like the one most people have in their homes.

Modern Language Association (MLA) Style: MLA style specifies guidelines for formatting and properly using the English language in writing papers for broad liberal arts and humanities courses especially. MLA style also provides a system for referencing your sources through parenthetical citation throughout your paper and on the final Works Cited pages.

Operating System: An operating system manages a computer's programs and hardware resources. To run applications on the computer, an operating system is necessary. The current operating system is Windows 7 for PCs and OS X for Macs.

Paraphrasing: Expressing ideas from another source in your own words. Even when using your own words, you need to credit the source of the ideas.

Plagiarism: To use another person's ideas or words without asking permission and/or giving credit. Plagiarism can be a blatant copy and paste of another author's ideas or exact words without formatting within quotation marks or crediting the author.

Random Access Memory (RAM): The place in a computer where the operating system, application programs, and data in current use are kept so that they can be quickly reached by the computer's processor. RAM can be compared to a person's short-term memory, while the computer's hard drive can be compared to the long-term memory. Rebooting your computer clears RAM.

Rubric: A rubric is a tool that helps you and your instructor assess your work and assign a grade on a particular project, paper, or a specific assignment. Generally, a rubric presents categories that make up the critical components of an assignment, such as understanding of specific course content, incorporation of supporting evidence, and basic writing skills. The components may be presented along a scale, with examples for inadequate, adequate, or exemplary work.

Scroll Bar: A graphical object that allows you to drag hidden portions of a screen into view. Some pages in your course will be too long or wide for you to view on your screen. You will find an area at the side or bottom of the screen that will allow you to move up and down or side-to-side on the page. Click on either arrow at the top/bottom or left/right of the scroll area, or click and drag the bar to view the page.

Search Engine: An Internet database program used for finding information. Yahoo! and Google are types of search engines.

Server: A computer that shares resources with client computers or links together computers in a network. Websites are stored on servers, and most businesses use one or more servers to keep employees connected.

Software: A general term for the various kinds of programs used to operate computers and related devices. Microsoft Word is an example of software. Some software is free.

Spammer: Someone who sends unsolicited e-mail.

Style Guide or Style Manual: Reference works that provide editing and formatting standards for use in academic papers.

Syllabus: An outline or summary of the main components or key information of a course of study.

Synchronous Course or Program: Program or course where the instructor and students must log into the online classroom environment at specified times and participate in the learning experience together. Instructors and students use the Internet to access an online classroom.

Thesis Statement: A statement of the main point or focus of your paper in the first paragraph.

Threaded Discussion: A virtual "board" where students and instructors can post and respond to comments or "threads" on any topic they choose.

Thumb Drive: (also called an external drive or jump drive) A portable storage device that can be connected to a computer via a USB port.

Uniform Resource Locator (URL): A website's address. Each website has a unique URL.

Vlog: A "video blog," where the owner/author of the website or blog uploads videos or videotaped messages to watch instead of typing out a written blog message, though there may be accompanying text.

Webinar: A seminar given via the web or live presentation on the Internet.

Website: One or more pages written in HyperText Markup Language (HTML) and stored on a web-accessible server that can be accessed through a unique URL. A website may contain text, images, video, audio, and interactive components. The first page of a website is referred to as the site's "home page." All websites combine to form the World Wide Web.

World Wide Web: (also referred to as the Web or WWW) A system for accessing information over the Internet. All of the different resources that people have made available through online servers form a giant web of information that can be accessed through web browsers. The web has been described as "the universe of network-accessible information; an embodiment of human knowledge." (retrieved from http://searchcrm.techtarget.com/definition/World-Wide-Web)

Online Resources

Below are some fundamental categories for resources that any student, but particularly an online student, might find useful. No matter how rapidly various online resources change, these categories will help provide a good start. From here, you can create your own checklist of resources and indispensible website bookmarks to access.

Online Search

Online search engines, such as Google, are a great way to find the websites you need. Enter a topic, a question, an organization, or a company to locate answers or web pages dedicated to countless topics. If a URL listed somewhere has changed or is not functioning, type the name or title of that site to get a more up-to-date page. For example, typing any of the software titles, websites, or organizations mentioned below should set you on the way to locating useful resources.

Hardware and Software

You most likely are using a PC or Macintosh® computer. And, there is a good chance that if you are using a PC, it is running some version of Microsoft Windows. To access support and other information for the type of computer and the software you are using, begin at the home pages for Microsoft or Apple Computer, Inc.

Firewall

Your computer may have a firewall already installed (but not necessarily activated). Likewise, some routers have built-in firewalls. However, if you determine that you need to acquire or install a firewall, there are free options available, such as ZoneAlarm®. Use an online search engine and enter the term "firewall" to learn more about current options for your operating system.

Virus Protection

Virus protection software is available for purchase, but often requires you to renew a subscription. There are also free virus protection software programs available, such as AVG Free. Use an online search engine and enter the term "virus protection software" to learn more about current options for your operating system.

Online Library

Explore your institution's online (or even on-the-ground) library, a valuable hub of information and resources. Libraries often contain more than books and articles, and librarians are there to help.

Online Writing Sites

There are many helpful online writing labs and resources free of charge. Even though some may be affiliated with a specific university, they offer plenty of tips and strategies applicable to any student. The OWL at Purdue is one well-known site. The Walden Writing Center is another site that features resources for undergraduate, graduate, and doctoral students, including tutorials and APA guidance.

If your institution has a writing center, locate its home page, bookmark it, and take advantage of its offerings, which may include tutoring. A writing center exists to support students who want to become better writers.

Student Support

Locate your institution's online support contact information. You may have access to e-mail, chat, or phone support. Also, locate your institution's "Frequently Asked Questions" or "FAQ" page, if available. These pages often provide the quick answer you may need.

Academic Writing Links

http://www.waldenwritingcenter.blogspot.com/
The Walden Writing Center Blog is a good resource, generic enough to be useful to anyone.

http://owl.english.purdue.edu/
The Purdue University OWL is considered one of the most comprehensive resources.

http://www.worldcat.org/
Worldcat can be really helpful with identifying resources and building sample citations.

http://www.ted.com/
TED talks are a good resource.

http://www.khanacademy.org
The Khan Academy, Inc. provides some interesting resources for students (for digging further).

Technology Links

Microsoft: http://www.microsoft.com
Apple: http://www.apple.com
Google: http://www.google.com

Trademarks and Disclaimers

"Adobe Acrobat" and "Flash" are both registered trademarks of Adobe Systems Inc. Adobe Systems Inc. is not affiliated with Laureate Education Inc., nor do they sponsor or endorse Laureate products or services.

"iPad, iPhone, iPod, Mac, Macintosh, QuickTime, and Safari" are all registered trademarks of Apple Computer, Inc. Apple Computer, Inc. is not affiliated with Laureate Education Inc., nor do they sponsor or endorse Laureate products or services.

"Shockwave" is a trademark of Atom Entertainment Inc. Atom Entertainment Inc. is not affiliated with Laureate Education Inc., nor do they sponsor or endorse Laureate products or services.

"BellSouth Corporation" is a registered trademark of AT&T Intellectual Property II, L.P. AT&T Intellectual Property II, L.P. is not affiliated with Laureate Education Inc., nor do they sponsor or endorse Laureate products or services.

"AntiVirus" and "AntiVirus FREE" are trademarks of AVG Technologies. AVG Technologies is not affiliated with Laureate Education Inc., nor do they sponsor or endorse Laureate products or services.

"ZoneAlarm" is a registered trademark of Check Point Software Technologies Inc. Check Point Software Technologies Inc. is not affiliated with Laureate Education Inc., nor do they sponsor or endorse Laureate products or services.

"Babson College" is a trademark of Entrepreneurship of All Kinds. Entrepreneurship of All Kinds is not affiliated with Laureate Education Inc., nor do they sponsor or endorse Laureate products or services.

"Android, Gmail, Google Books, Google Chrome, Google Docs, Google Scholar, and YouTube" are all trademarks of Google Inc. Google Inc. is not affiliated with Laureate Education Inc., nor do they sponsor or endorse Laureate products or services.

"McAfee" is a registered trademark of Intel. Intel is not affiliated with Laureate Education Inc., nor do they sponsor or endorse Laureate products or services.

"Norton" is a trademark of McAfee Inc. McAfee Inc. is not affiliated with Laureate Education Inc., nor do they sponsor or endorse Laureate products or services.

"Project Gutenberg" is a trademark of Michael S. Hart. Michael S. Hart is not affiliated with Laureate Education Inc., nor do they sponsor or endorse Laureate products or services.

"Excel, Internet Explorer, Office, Outlook, PowerPoint, Skype, Windows, Windows Media Player, and Word" are all registered trademarks of Microsoft Corporation. Microsoft Corporation is not affiliated with Laureate Education Inc., nor do they sponsor or endorse Laureate products or services.

"Moodle" is a trademark of Moodle Trust. Moodle Trust is not affiliated with Laureate Education Inc., nor do they sponsor or endorse Laureate products or services.

"Firefox" is a registered trademark of Mozilla Foundation. Mozilla Foundation is not affiliated with Laureate Education Inc., nor do they sponsor or endorse Laureate products or services.

"Open Directory Project" is a trademark of Netscape Communications Corp. Netscape Communications Corp. is not affiliated with Laureate Education Inc., nor do they sponsor or endorse Laureate products or services.

"WorldCat" is a trademark of OCLC, Inc. OCLC, Inc. is not affiliated with Laureate Education Inc., nor do they sponsor or endorse Laureate products or services.

"Java" is a trademark of Oracle America, Inc. Oracle America, Inc. is not affiliated with Laureate Education Inc., nor do they sponsor or endorse Laureate products or services.

"BlackBerry" is a registered trademark of Research In Motion Limited. Research In Motion Limited is not affiliated with Laureate Education Inc., nor do they sponsor or endorse Laureate products or services.

"Verizon" is a trademark of Verizon Trademark Services, LLC. Verizon Trademark Services, LLC is not affiliated with Laureate Education Inc., nor do they sponsor or endorse Laureate products or services.

"Hotmail" is a registered trademark of Yahoo!, Inc. Yahoo!, Inc. is not affiliated with Laureate Education Inc., nor do they sponsor or endorse Laureate products or services.

American Psychological Association, Blackboard Inc., Charter Communications Holding Company, LLC, Detroit Lions, Khan Academy, Inc., Milwaukee Brewers, Modern Language Association, Purdue University, TED, and Twitter Inc. are all not affiliated with Laureate Education Inc., nor do they sponsor or endorse Laureate products or services.

Index

A

B

C

I

J

K

L

M

P

Q

R

S

T